T0063489

UNDER THE SPELL

What if the notions you have about God and yourself are based on a lie?

JOHN DAVID

Copyright © 2021 John David.

All rights reserved. No part of this book may be used or reproduced by any means, graphic, electronic, or mechanical, including photocopying, recording, taping or by any information storage retrieval system without the written permission of the author except in the case of brief quotations embodied in critical articles and reviews.

WestBow Press books may be ordered through booksellers or by contacting:

WestBow Press
A Division of Thomas Nelson & Zondervan
1663 Liberty Drive
Bloomington, IN 47403
www.westbowpress.com
844-714-3454

Because of the dynamic nature of the Internet, any web addresses or links contained in this book may have changed since publication and may no longer be valid. The views expressed in this work are solely those of the author and do not necessarily reflect the views of the publisher, and the publisher hereby disclaims any responsibility for them.

Any people depicted in stock imagery provided by Getty Images are models, and such images are being used for illustrative purposes only.
Certain stock imagery © Getty Images.

Scripture taken from the New King James Version® Copyright © 1982 by Thomas Nelson. Used by permission. All rights reserved.

Scripture taken from the King James Version of the Bible.

Scripture quotations are from the ESV® Bible (The Holy Bible, English Standard Version®), copyright © 2001 by Crossway, a publishing ministry of Good News Publishers. Used by permission. All rights reserved.

ISBN: 978-1-6642-3184-9 (sc)
ISBN: 978-1-6642-3183-2 (e)

Print information available on the last page.

WestBow Press rev. date: 05/25/2021

I dedicate this is to the person God used to bring me to Jesus. You inspire me daily. And to my children. I hope you find and keep the truth. Lastly, to my dear friend Pastor Dave Browning, you are missed more than I can express.

CONTENTS

What if ...
we heard and told
the Truth, instead of old
familiar lies?

PREFACE

This book was written for those who were raised with the message that they were unwanted, alone, unworthy, and broken somehow. It's for people who have tried to be "okay" through professional success; exhausted themselves chasing acceptance; or compromised how they really feel and not spoken their mind in order to fit in. It's for those who wrestle with co-dependency, addiction, misuse of sexuality, or anxiety – those who feel numb or live in silent despair.

It's also for those who are spiritually inclined but are turned off by what they know of as Christianity – for people who struggle with words like evil, wicked, and sin – for those who don't subscribe to narrow-minded exclusionism or hypocrisy.

If you feel called to follow Jesus and want to explore the concepts taught in the Bible on a deeper level or want to reconcile the contradictions you see in the Bible, this is absolutely for you.

It's for you if you can relate to this…you said a version of the salvation prayer, and invited Christ into your heart. You've been attending church, and maybe you even got baptized, but nothing's changed. You still feel just as messed up as you did before. You still think and do selfish things, your life is still filled with problems, worry, and stress. You have wondered if this whole salvation thing is something you can't have. "Maybe God doesn't want me or maybe He wants to love me, but I'm just not lovable," you think. You worry that you're not worth saving, you've made too many mistakes, or the ones you made were too grave. You read the Bible and when you don't understand or something doesn't make sense, you ask your pastor(s), but their responses, while sounding nice, don't clear up any of your confusion. You pray, but you have no idea if how you're praying will work, and you're not sure what God's will is for you.

This book was written for you if you want to live in a world where fear, hate and violence aren't humanity's primary expressions, and you are willing to stand against them for the sake of future generations.

My hope is that reading it inspires you to take a fresh look at the Bible, exposes you to some ideas, methods, and tools to enhance your personal exploration of Truth, and of God's life-giving instructions. I hope that you have lots of ah ha! moments where things become clear and make sense.

If what Scripture says is true, then you really are loved for who you are, as you are. You are enough, and you have been chosen to spread this truth across humanity.

> *The Bible is true. So you are loved, valuable, taken care of, and made on purpose to be an expression of God's love.*

When I initially felt compelled to write this book, I envisioned addressing a few core misconceptions around Christianity and getting into an advanced "what's in the Bible" dialogue with the hope of stimulating some interest in further exploration of scripture. At best, I hoped to open up a few minds closed off to the idea of checking it out. As I prayed for direction, the scope broadened, at which point I imagined that the task at hand would be in studying, learning about, and then articulating a synthesis of information and concepts from scholarly works across ancient world views to include a diverse range of philosophy, current science, the works of psychology, and theology, while attempting to reach the inner-person of the reader. My goal was to get past the ego to the soul, awakening remembrance or sparking a recollection of the truth. What I found perplexing was trying to do so to a mixed audience of opposing views without offending or turning people off, while at the same time, not compromising truth (as I understand and believe it to be).

The question I asked myself was, "How do I talk to non-believers, atheists, and agnostics about the truth in Scripture, when "Christianity" is such a loaded word and concept? How do I point out the historically errant and violent ways of the institutionalized church and their misappropriation of Scripture without offending those affiliated with such organizations today? How do I share what I've personally experienced and learned about Scripture without coming across as a heretic to theologians and evangelicals who are often quick to label "unorthodox teaching" as "false?" How do I expose the "un-scientific" theories of science, talk to a selfish nation about greed and how our "all-or-nothing" rationale has contributed to the downfall of humanity without offending the majority? The answer is simple — I don't. While I might be speaking to a mixed audience with opposing views — and initiating dialogue about controversial subjects — this book is ultimately about **my beliefs, my experience,** and **my truth** about Scripture and how it relates to humans today. It's ultimately up to readers to decide for themselves what they believe to be true and how they wish to respond.

Over the years, I've read countless books on religious philosophy, including books about Judaism, Buddhism, Confucianism, Taoism, Hinduism, the Mexican Toltec, Native American writings, and the Muslim Koran. I've studied ancient civilizations, their histories, customs, beliefs, and gods, with a special focus on sects operating in the Middle East. I've read and studied the diverse views of philosophy, including Parmenides vs. Heraclitus, Plato and Aristotle, Lao Tzu, Kung Fu Tzu, Chaung Tzu and Huai Nan Tzu, Kierkegaard, Pascal, Descartes, Marx, Hue, Rousseau, Russell, Nietzsche, and Voltaire. I've studied Cognitive Behavioral Therapy, rewiring the brain, psychology in general and the works of Freud, Lacan, Jung, Gutama, Freil and countless others. I've explored and researched anthropology and archaeological discoveries; studied physics (classic, atomic, subatomic and nuclear), new science, paranormal phenomena, past life regressions, and the study of DNA, relationships and recovery.

I'm grateful I've been trained to "look for similarities — not differences," because what I've discovered is that when you look past these differences, what you see is a common theme coming from different perspectives. Almost all of the writings I mention above, though very different, support an integrated truth of a Divine Being, a Power greater than the human ego and the truth about God.

Because of my personal experiences, there is no room for doubt, no intelligible argument; nor could a persuasive case be made to change what I believe to be true about God, my existence, and my purpose. From early on, my private self seemed acutely aware of my soul's presence. I would describe it as if I've always known that "I" (my core self) am somehow lost and on a quest, searching for clues in order to find my way home. Sometimes it felt like I had amnesia, but I knew it. Interestingly enough, I was not psychologically or socially conditioned to believe in Christianity, but rather the opposite. Yet my inner person was strangely familiar with the concept of God, eternity, my soul, the truth about my spiritual family, and myself.

For years I viewed "Christianity" as "glorified hypocrisy" and thought that its followers, much like sheep being led to the slaughter, were morons. Interestingly enough, I joined the movement decades later after what I can only describe as a divine redirection (a story I will later share). My conversion to Christianity first manifested itself intellectually, with the belief that Jesus was the model that we as humans should all strive to emulate. My faith grew as I began to participate in the church community, discipleship, and ministry, but more recently, it was my encounter with the Holy Spirit that grounded my faith and cemented my belief about the Bible's teachings and the truth about God and my relationship with Him. If you don't consider yourself a Christian, don't let my "Christian terminology" (i.e. Holy Spirit, discipleship, or ministry) disturb you. For the most part, this book is written in plain English, but there are times when Bible terms are the only words that can accurately describe my experience and/or point.

I think it's important to shift gears and establish context for how this book came about. It's relevant to you as a reader to know more about me, my circumstances and why for the past several years I've spent up to 14 hours a day studying Scripture and countless other works pointing to the truth about God. I am not a religious zealot, philosopher or theologian. I was leading men's ministry at a church, married, and raising 4 stepchildren while working in the software industry. I have the disease of alcoholism and wasn't active in a program of recovery. I relapsed, ended up in jail, lost my wife, and my job. Eventually my struggle with alcohol led me to prison. Once there I started 'really' reading the Bible, which grew into a progressive study of the scriptures, their contents, and their origin.

I read the writings of various scholars and theologians dating back to the Patristic-Medieval era up to the Post Reformation, including the works of Augustine, Pelican, Aquinas, Sibley, Luther, Calvin, Spurgeon, Chautard, Wesley, Edwards, Tillich, R.C. Sproul, Swindoll, C.S. Lewis and many more. I studied the motivations behind Pantheism, Panentheism, and Deism as alternative views to Theism. I researched the history of the Catholic Church dating back to the second century, its establishment, its doctrine, and the role that the council played in its rise to power and influence.

Here is the conclusion I came to. The Scripture of the Old and New Testament in the original writings (manuscripts) are the inspired word of God. This by no means suggests that men, even religious men, have not at times misappropriated, misinterpreted or perverted its meanings, for they most certainly have. Christ is the authority on the interpretation of all Scripture. If our understanding is not in line with His teaching, then we don't have the correct understanding. Today, I don't merely believe that there is a God and that Jesus exists. I **truly believe** that **everything** Jesus said and taught is the absolute truth. I believe that His instruction, while brief, is packed with meaning. It is comprehensive and complete. It is the roadmap for the salvation of humanity, for social justice and peace on earth. I believe He modeled every aspect of how we should live, from how to relate to God and others, to how to confront and resist evil. He demonstrated how to love others in tangible ways and how to use our spiritual gifts to help heal the world one person, one power, or one institution at a time.

In addition, I believe He called us into action. He didn't condone complacency, or merely being content with our personal salvation. He instructed us to share what we have, to right our wrongs, to defend the weak, and to feed the poor. He told us to share the truth about His nature and about our existence as His spiritual children. He did not teach passivity, but rather taught love, non-violence, and the resistance of evil. He spoke out against materialism, domination, selfishness, oppression, and injustice. He called out lying, cheating, stealing, and hypocrisy. Jesus opposed marginalizing groups or individuals, and was against prejudice and against judgment. He taught that you and I are no better or worse than our neighbor, and most importantly, He taught forgiveness.

I believe that there is exuberant joy and beauty to be found for each of us when we express God's creative love. I also believe that as hard as it is, love involves respecting an individual's choices. Thus Christ will never "force" any of us to do the right thing (hence the problem with evil).

1

WHAT ARE WE TALKING ABOUT?

Jesus came to expose the lie, but society could not comprehend

JOHN 1:15

The state of our world is very troubling, and our efforts to ignore, deny, or justify the truth about how poorly humans are treating each other **do not work**. Subconsciously, we are all affected by the mistreatment of others and the injustice and corruption all around us, and pay a price directly or indirectly.

Many of us view ourselves as powerless to effect meaningful change at a group level. Many have given away individual and collective authority to create positive conditions for everyone, and are focused on the worlds we define for ourselves with immediate family and friends, the identities we create through the roles we play, and what we post on Facebook, Twitter, and Instagram. We are focused on short-term gratification, and if we were honest with ourselves, we would acknowledge that in the back of our minds we lack hope for the future of humanity.

Our society teaches us to be independent, that we should have the "willpower" and determination to achieve anything on our own. We are taught that being dependent is a negative thing, because it means not having control over our own destiny or freedom in our life. Worse, it means being dominated by the thing (or person) on which we are dependent. This teaching is not only false, but also, it is the basis for all of our problems (all of humanity's problems). Our notion of self, the ego (Greek for "I"), is that "I am a separate person," an individual. All of this is a lie, a distortion or departure from the truth about our nature and existence. Our false notion of separateness and independence is deeply rooted in humanity's misconception of existence.

Most of us can see plenty of evidence that we alone are not calling the shots in life. At best, with great determination, we are influencing them, but not always in our favor or in the best interests of others. Many people are unaware that the true meaning of the word individual is "undivided," so in truth we are not separated, but are a bunch of undivideds. In actuality, we are all connected, and entirely "dependent" on the source of existence to sustain us mentally, physically, and spiritually.

Our existence as a species, hence our identity, is one of the most important topics we could learn about, and yet it is so perplexing that most of us avoid thinking about it altogether.

Every fear, every one of our destructive behaviors, all self-doubt, vanity, guilt, or emotional problems we have – all greed, pride, selfishness, violence, and misuse of sexuality, is directly tied to what we think and believe about existence.

As a society, we perpetuate the lie that personal success has to do with "achieving." We are taught that in pursuing wealth, financial security, popularity, or acceptance, we will become okay, when in fact doing so has the opposite effect. We place our trust in (worship) acquiring things, to be okay, to fill the emptiness inside, and to give ourselves a sense of security, money, possessions, romance, acceptance, information – personal power), and as we either achieve or fail to reach our goals with these things, we are quietly (subconsciously) perplexed that they don't work. We try harder, we try the next thing society says will work…more alcohol, drugs, sex, gambling, shopping, and over-eating…a new spouse…and nothing works for long. Subconsciously, we feel defeated, confused, and hopeless. We become more fearful, and in turn more selfish.

Truth: We will not find peace, happiness, or joy through the accumulation of more possessions and wealth or in posting storyboards of happy lives on social media (false imagery). The majority of humanity has been deceived. Most of us have just accepted the beliefs society promotes without any real thought or analysis. As a society, our notions of existence, of God (if you believe), of ourselves as physical beings, and of what success is, **are distorted**.

Historically, as an institution, the Church has missed Christ's mark. Pictures of an untrustworthy God have been subversively represented through many theological doctrines. The spiritual truths and instructions contained in the Bible have at times been misrepresented. As a result, unbeknownst to them, many "Christians" are not actually following the teachings (doctrine) of Christ. In fact, a small number of those professing to be Christians truly study the Bible, and after the first century, as we will see, Christianity started becoming something different from what Jesus taught and modeled.

There remains today a fog of deception across society that keeps us from clearly seeing the truth. My intention is to shine a light on it, to show people some things they're not aware of, and how knowing it can make all the difference between being okay and not being okay.

In the pages that follow, we will explore truths and some subtle but major misconceptions about existence, about who or what God is, about the principles that guide our universe, about humans in relation to all of it – and about perfect love. We will look at what science, psychology, and the Bible **actually** say about us, in contrast to the common notion's society projects. We will investigate belief, and the meaning of words like sin, evil, wicked, death, salvation, and prayer – as well as look at what Christianity is meant to be.

Before we get going, there are some ideas about you and me to consider. The first is about the process of abstraction and our mental map. We first start compiling a map of symbols and the words of our language in childhood, with little analysis, so they are not clearly defined and have several meanings. As a result, we may misunderstand some words and incorrectly assume their meanings to be other than they are. Then when it comes to an English translation of the Bible, we really can't "assume" the meanings of words at all. Several factors come into play, from things like how the translators viewed the task of translation, to changes in the use of English words over the centuries, to the individual filters through which each of us run information.

For example, in the original Hebrew and Greek manuscripts there are at least fifteen specific terms that when translated into English were assigned the generic word "love." More times than not, numerous terms with different meanings got condensed into single English words, leaving room for assumed meaning and misinterpretation. Then there's the fact that the original scriptures were written thousands of years ago in ancient languages that recognize spiritual and material as the inner and outer aspects of things, and the fact that while there are concrete stories about physical happenings, the "teachings" in the Bible are about spiritual or mental things; about our thoughts, beliefs, and states of mind, not concrete things.

Second, as children, we fall from our natural perception of things around age five, as we start getting socialized. So each of our views are shaped, not by what we naturally experience and observe, but by the messages society and our family give us growing up, the same society that Jesus says is ruled by the spirit of lies, distortions, and accusations.

Third, "reality" is truly a matter of perception. What we think and believe, and our perceptions of the experiences we've had, are the filters through which we formulate our conscious world or mind (city in the Old Testament). **Actuality**, on the other hand, is truth, "what is," regardless of how one filters it.

For you and me, <u>everything</u> boils down to what we allow or disallow to shape our reality. This is where the ultimate use of free will occurs, where the Bible instructs us to "take our thoughts captive," how to "renew our minds," and how to pray as a means of overcoming fear ("the lie").

Most of us don't spend much time learning about what we (human beings) are, and how we work, but from the most basic and scientific perspective, we are **energy directed by thought.**

An inner dialogue of fear, unworthiness, abandonment, or shame can translate to debilitating defeat, because it's not just thoughts and beliefs that paralyze a person, but changes in the blood chemistry throughout the entire body, within every cell. When you have negative (fearful) thoughts, the immune system shuts down, digestion stops working properly, and your cognitive thinking functions (reasoning) take a backseat to the subconscious mind, which out of reflex reacts to alarms, based on our false beliefs, and distorted perceptions about the meaning of events or situations. If you think you can't, you won't. If you believe you can, eventually you will!

As a result of all of this, many of us are unknowingly driven by a negative internal dialogue and worry (fear) which leads to self-destructive behavior and emotional, mental, and physical and premature death. **Our misdirected pursuit of security leads to our destruction**.

Fourth, the teachings of the Bible, psychology, and philosophy are all focused on our mental consciousness, on what we think. There's the foreground, our conscious mind; the background, processing which happens in the subconscious mind, and the intuitive mind, which some call the unconscious. Your memories and beliefs are stored in the subconscious mind, which governs about 95% of what you do.

WHAT DO YOU LONG FOR?

- Do you want to feel complete and filled with purpose?
- Would you like to live a balanced life, and have healthy relationships (with yourself, with others, and with money)?
- Do you want serenity, peace of spirit, mental and physical health?
- Do you want to love others well, and feel loved?

Everything happens for a reason...success is not an accident, it's predictable. Failure is not an accident. **Truth:** our success in life is most heavily influenced by what we allow ourselves to think and believe, not by circumstances or conditions as we often assume. Many of us do not truly understand this.

The absolute truth is that we are not helpless, and it's not too late for humanity, but we need to change how we think. We can operate as we are designed to, our beliefs, thoughts, and actions can become expressions of love, creative intelligence and selflessness—expressions of God. You can be complete, filled with purpose, and full of love. **This is exactly what the Bible (when understood) teaches us to do.**

We are told, "Do not be shaped by society's beliefs, values, and trends; instead be changed by the renovation of your mind, so that by testing you can prove what is the choice of God, what is fully agreeable, what fits, and what reaches the goal of complete mental growth." – Romans 12:2 (author's literal translation).

The "cloud of deception" that the Bible says society operates under makes it difficult to see some of the messages in the Bible. Our belief becomes clearer and clearer as we study scripture, and the Holy Spirit teaches us. And our faith becomes stronger and stronger as we apply what we've learned. The more involved we are with this process, the more things become crystallized. We see things we missed before.

Be a Spell Breaker!

2

SEEKING TRUTH – ACTUALITY

"Falsehood has an infinity of combinations,
but truth has only one mode of being."

JEAN-JACQUES ROUSSEAU

Before we get into what we think about God or about ourselves, let's each take a moment to step back and get clear on what we think about existence, about the universe, about the world we live in, and about how it works. For a lot of us, our understanding of these things is filtered through vague notions and beliefs we've been fed, rather than any conscious effort to think critically and analyze information about them.

What are your thoughts about these things and what are the sources which formed your understanding? What did you learn in high school or college vs. what you've just picked up over the course of your life — from what is portrayed in movies or on TV — or what you have validated through direct experience in observing and relating to the environment around you?

Do you think of things in terms of what is concrete, what you can rationalize? Does the world around us consist of empty space and solid objects, for example, the rooms in our house in which we put furniture? Is time something absolute, something you can count on? Or do you think in a less confined manner, wondering about things like whether the past is simply a way of breaking up the experience we are having to focus on certain aspects, i.e., our concept of time coupled with memory is our way of indexing the experience of being so that we can hit pause, rewind, replay, and fast-forward? Or that perhaps the past is somewhere else?

There's what we think of as **reality**, rational knowledge, the intellectual map we construct on which we discern, divide, contrast, compare, measure, and categorize things. Then there's what is, the multidimensional **actuality** where things have inner and outer characteristics and go together; where things cannot always be separated or explained, but rather are encountered through direct experiences, frequently beyond the five senses (taste, touch, smell, hearing, sight).

According to science today, we don't operate in a three-dimensional world. Our common understanding of solid material objects is false. Space is not empty, there is no absolute time. We can't always split large things into smaller parts to arrive at an explanation. Those common concepts, however, are deeply engrained in our habits of thought, so it's extremely difficult to imagine a physical reality where they don't apply.

In truth, the idea of seeing everything as separate is a manifestation of "the lie." For example, in the 1930s it was known that all matter consisted of atoms and that all atoms consisted of protons, neutrons, and electrons. These were thought of as elementary particles, the "basic building blocks" of matter. Today, there are no base building blocks. We know of hundreds of particles and understand the properties (other entities) that help form particles as being constituents. Today, science understands that "rational inquiry" doesn't work as the exclusive mode of scientific observation.

Dynamic energy bundles form stable nuclear, atomic, and molecular structures that build up matter, providing us with the illusion of a solid aspect, making us believe that it is made of some material substance. Today, scientists understand that atoms consist of vast regions of space in which extremely small dynamic energy packets move around. These bundles of energy can be dual in nature, sometimes appearing as waves, and sometimes as particles, depending on how we look at them. What we call a particle is an energy bundle confined or condensed to a small region of space — and a wave is the energy spread out over a large region of space. When the energy is confined to a small volume, it moves around — the smaller the space, the faster the movement. An electron confined in an atom results in vibrating velocities of 600 miles per second — giving matter its illusion of a solid aspect.

I do not wish to make your head hurt in thinking about things that might feel overwhelming, but here's another very fundamental thread of information to share. Modern physics has defined what is called a Quantum Field, "a fundamental physical entity that is a continuous medium which is present everywhere in space." Particles then are merely local concentrations of energy that come and go, dissolving into the underlying field, not static or permanent, but dynamic and transitory. In other words, everything that is forms through this ever-present medium, then at some point un-forms and returns into it. Science has essentially come full circle back to the ancient Greek school of thought. The Greek Milesian School that founded physics, "the study of seeing the essential nature or real constitution of things," used the word "pneuma," meaning "current," "breath," or "ether," to describe what in the English Bible is termed "spirit." The ancient Chinese philosophies of life [Taoism, Confucianism, and neo-Confucianism, which incorporates Buddhism], use the word "chi" when talking about what is "the essence of all material objects." "Chi," literally translated, means "ether" or gas, "the vital breath."

Let your thoughts about all of this sit in the background as we move on to what God is and what we are.

3

WHO'S GOD – WHOSE GOD

"Happy is the man who finds wisdom, And the man who gains understanding."

PROVERBS 3:13

I vividly remember a conversation I had with my mother when I was five. It was a sunny weekday morning. I was in the front yard and my mom was on the porch. I remember a sequence of events: it was beautiful outside, the sky was bright blue with a slight haze, the birds were chirping, the air smelled of roses and spring, and there were flowers everywhere. I glanced at an orange flower with a bee buzzing around it, then noticed a beautiful butterfly, and went into one of those temporary trance-like states, you know, when you are gazing intensely, but not at any one thing, and you have soft eyes and see everything at the same time peripherally. People call it staring off into space. I was completely aware of everything around me (cars, street noise, dogs, birds, etc.), and paying attention to it all at the same time, when it seemed to blend. There was kind of a momentary freeze frame, and for a millisecond I saw a snapshot of it all and realized that everything was part of one thing. While this was happening, I blurted out something about "You know, Mom, God is nature." My mom responded and I looked up at her, but before I made sense of the words she was saying, I noticed a sweet smile and a whimsical expression on her face. It was transparent, a combination of surprise and curiosity. She was asking me a question, "John, do you believe in God?" I remember the inflection in her voice. I proceeded to tell her that God was the Sun, the Moon, and the Ocean, and that Jesus was real, and "our purpose was to learn to love better." I hadn't been taught about Jesus, my parents weren't Christian or religious, and no one was speaking to me about God at that age.

Then I remember another day, while I was waiting in my room for my dad to give me my second ever spanking, I was crying and actually praying out loud to God, "God, please help me," "God, please protect me," "I promise I will never do it again, God." I don't know if things like this happened for you, but it's really strange at the age of five to talk to God in a time of trouble, out of instinct, when you live in a household where the word God is never used. Or maybe it's not so strange at all? Little children aren't tarnished or corrupt in thought, they have innocence and purity, they trust truth, and they don't yet know disbelief.

> Jesus said... ***"Assuredly, I say to you, whoever does not receive the kingdom of God as a little child [new believer] will by no means enter it."*** [Luke 18:17].

My parents got divorced later that year, and there was a period of turmoil. I don't remember too much thought about God for a few years. When I was nine, the house my mother, my sister, and I lived in was in a neighborhood of mostly graduate and theology students. There were several theology colleges right there at the edge of the U.C. Berkeley campus. I used to play football on their grass fields and remember how special the place felt. A new kid from Georgia, Michael, moved in next door, and we became friends. His father was a pastor on temporary assignment over the summer at a church a couple of blocks away. I was invited to church one day and went. I didn't meet Michael in the Sunday school as planned, but instead went into the adult sanctuary to check out the service. I was curious about why people went to church and what they did there. I went a few more times more before Michael moved away. Then, about two years later, when I was 11, I decided to try another church just a few blocks in the other direction. I got dressed in a suit, went alone, and sat sandwiched in between what I thought of as old people. It was difficult to follow along with the rituals that everyone but me seemed to know: when to sit, when to stand, and how to find the right page for prayers or songs. I remember disliking the organ music, and thinking the songs were pretty dull, and yet the act of standing and singing (corporate worship) was deeply moving. Again, I didn't care for the music at all, couldn't find the words to sing, and was embarrassed and tired of standing, but I was deeply moved.

THE MISCONCEPTIONS

Now, by my teens, I lived in a different neighborhood, and growing up in a diverse, multi-cultural university town, not many of the people I knew bought into organized religion. I had formed stereotypes about evangelists, and like all prejudice, mine was born out of ignorance. I'd made generalizations from what I saw of televangelists on TV and movies, as well as from the endless visits that the Jehovah's Witnesses made to our door. I unfairly lumped them into two categories: con men who faked healings for personal gain, and the lost fools who listened to and funded them.

We all have our own ideas of what God might be. For some people the word "God" has negative connotations for various reasons, but by and large, most people have the belief that there is something greater than ourselves, something that makes it all work.

Non-religious people most frequently say things like they believe in a connected universe or universal laws like Karma, that God is the energy that powers it all, and interestingly, almost everyone imagines that God has to do with love. Funny, that's what the Bible says, too!

From my experience working in leadership positions at church, I know that Christians often have significant misconceptions about different religions and their gods, as do others about Christianity. Even the word "God" has different meanings depending on whom you're speaking with. Before we dive into our discussion about God, let's gain a bit of clarity about and context around some of the differences.

Buddhism is not a religion, and Buddha is not a god. A man name Siddhartha Gautama wrote down his epiphanies on applying acceptance and humility to day-to-day living as a means of overcoming mental suffering. It is a psychological philosophy of how to live in acceptance, balance, and harmony, not in conflict with ourselves and the rest of creation.

The Chinese ways of life in Confucianism and Taoism are wisdom-based frameworks for living, statements of the cause and effect of human action as it relates to the natural laws of energy, and being a part of a harmonious flow, rather than resisting things. For the most part, the various religious mythologies of the world, be they Babylonian, Egyptian, Greek, Hindu, or Nordic gods, are actually not about different gods, but rather the same cast of characters known in the Bible as fallen angels. Archaeological excavations in the Middle East over the last 150 years have shown us that there was one spoken and written language prior to the scattering of people, as stated in the biblical account of the "Tower of Babel." We can see in the

Sumerian history books and records the names of "those cast down from heaven." One key find was the massive Assyrian library dug up with the city of Nineveh. In it were dictionaries and lexicons to the ancient Sumerian cuneiform tablets found in the 1840s in Sumer, or Ur, where Abraham was born, modern-day Baghdad in Iraq, to translate them into Akkadian, the precursor language to ancient Aramaic and Hebrew. We can see the names of some fallen angels as they started in Sumerian cuneiform, then as they changed from Akkadian into various languages that evolved as people migrated to India, the Nordic regions, Russia, and Greece. The Hindu gods Shiva, Kumar and Anup, the Greek gods Zeus, Athena and Apollo, and the Norse gods like Thor, Odin, etc. are the same celestial beings (angels) who were worshiped as 'gods' in Genesis 6 of the Bible.

The Biblical account of creation involves one Source of energy creating all things that were inherently good. The fall of man, hence evil (wrong thought) came through believing a lie. By contrast, the Babylonian creation story (from which the other religions originated) is one where a father god is killed by one of his rebellious sons (Marduk) who then murders the mother god in violent fashion, tearing her carcass apart to create the cosmos and using the blood drops from her corpse to create humans to serve the gods. The mother (Tiamat) was supposed to represent chaos, and through her death, order was restored. This is where the myths that violence saves, that wars can bring peace, and that good guys killing bad guys are heroes come from; the origin of "redemptive violence," "just wars," and the "hero complex." It's also the basis for religious codes and societal views that subjugate women.

Trying to define God absolutely would be limiting. However, we can gain a working knowledge of God's nature through the Bible, which deals with exactly that.

The world we live in projects a lot of false or at least spiritually limited notions about the concepts taught in the Bible. Let's look at some of these typical misconceptions:

- God = Supreme superhuman power from above who imposes His laws on earth. You and I had better fear getting on his bad side.
- Existence = The physical world.
- Mankind = Physical beings, flesh and blood. We live, then we die.
- Soul = Something "some people" believe in; the spirit
- Salvation = When we verbally accept Christ as our savior, we are granted eternal life with God. It means that when we die, our soul doesn't burn in hell.
- Heaven = The place where we go, if we're good, after our physical death. Probably in outer space.
- Prayer = We make a request up to the sky, hoping somehow that God receives it.

Notions along these lines lead to some drastic misconceptions about what the Bible is telling us, and in turn, sometimes what people teach us.

WHO'S GOD?

The first thing to realize is that God in the Bible is not simply a superior version of man with superpowers and great wisdom, nor is God merely a raw force of energy. Both are common misconceptions.

The Bible says that God is the truth, the source of all creation and the endless universe (existence, life, all that is) of the abundance that we see through telescopes, the infinite variety we encounter through microscopes, and all we are still unaware of.

God is the beginning and the end. God is infinite, unsearchable, incomparable, all-knowing, impartial, consistent, and eternal. God is not just life-giving, but is life itself, existence. God is the pneuma, the spirit, the energy (chi, quantum field) of all things. God is not just "loving," but is love itself. God is intelligence and creativity. God is Principal.

One main challenge we have in discussing God is that there is no adequate pronoun to use. God is not a person in the normal sense, but trying to use something like "it" would imply an inanimate and unintelligent object, and would lack reverence. We use "He" and "Him," which makes sense in that God is relational and Jesus was male and used the euphuism of Father when describing the proper parent-child relationship we should have with God. However, the Bible says that God created both males and females as his images and likenesses, so God is not exclusively male. I kind of like the way the author of *The Shack* described God because it got me thinking about how loving, caring, and nurturing God is (the feminine traits).

Along these same lines, God is not "out there" somewhere. He's everywhere. Actually, He's inside of you. At least the aspect of God we communicate with is. He is reached through our minds (hearts). In the Book of Luke verses 17:20-21, Jesus said, "The kingdom of God is within you," using the Greek word "entros," meaning "inside." He also said that we should seek first the kingdom of God, or that we should be all about finding God inside of us, and everything else needed would follow.

The DNA that is the same in all living things, that is God. The spirit of God literally abides in us.

The Bible is teaching us about becoming aware of the actual presence of God within us. He is the light and the electricity. We are meant to be the lightbulbs, so to speak—the bright reflections of His spirit.

There are so many misconceptions that stand in the way of each of us exploring our Divine purpose and learning about the true nature of God. It's as if we are all under a spell separating us from reality.

I have had countless conversations with people who say that they believe in God, or at least that there is one, but who are reluctant about believing in Christianity. Each of these people has agreed that from what they know of Jesus, he would be the ideal loving person for all to emulate. Some, however, feel that His followers, "Christians," are exclusionists, who live selfish lives filled with hypocrisy and material focus, who have a superficial awareness of the world around them, ambivalence toward the needy and the hopeless, and very little engagement. Sadly, I agree that more often than not there is truth to some of these observations about people. I would submit, however, that we are talking about people in general, and not Christ followers. The true Christ-following families whom I know are the salt of the earth; they care for each other and extend their love to strangers, often opening their homes or literally selling their material possessions so that strangers won't have to "go without."

Not all who call themselves Christian are in fact followers of Christ. That is a big misconception. I don't think people are intentionally lying, they just don't know any better. Some identify with Christianity through cultural inheritance, and that's where their faith stops, while others are raised "Christian," but are not living out Christ's teachings. In both cases there may be fairly significant misconceptions of what it means to believe in Christ. Jesus did not ask anyone to "identify" with Christianity; rather, He suggested that those who wished to follow Him should consider the high cost. He stated that those who believed would forsake themselves and their old lives, and follow Him in a life-long journey to become selfless and more loving; actually, becoming divine expressions of God. It seems like a huge sacrifice, one that most don't understand and very few are willing to make.

Many misunderstand the core teachings of the Bible. Christians are not supposed to sit passively in suffering, waiting for God to personally fix humanity or thump us on our heads with "His will." We are called to develop and use our spiritual gifts, to not only "let" God work through us, but also to "ask" Him to work miracles through us in changing all that is wrong in the world. We are to live as beacons of His light.

Much of what Jesus taught had to do with loving fellow humans, feeding the hungry, and sharing what you have. In fact, He said that you were not one of His people if you didn't care for the least of your fellows. Eighty-five percent of Americans say they believe in God, and yet forty-nine million people in the U.S. don't have enough food to feed all of their family members. I guess within these families people take turns eating.

A survey done in Russia showed that fifty-two percent [52%] of the people who identified themselves as Orthodox Christians said they have never read 'any' part of the Bible. In today's newspaper, I read that the Russian government recently destroyed 350 tons of food... the food was burned and steamrolled following a decree by President Vladimir Putin that products from Europe and the United States be banned.

Another related misconception, though, is that along with the realization of God's existence and a conscious decision to "believe" comes immediate and lasting change in a person. In other words, he believes, has been baptized, and we go to church, so now he will act "Godly." All humans have a selfish aspect (ego), and at times will err in that way, Christian and non-Christian alike. I've learned this the hard way! "*...If we say that we have no sin, we deceive ourselves and the truth is not in us.*" –1 John 1:8.

Baptism is certainly an important part of starting a new life, but it is just the tip of the iceberg, the jumping-off point. What exactly does this person believe in? That Jesus existed, or that "everything" He taught us about existence, His nature as God, and our nature is true?

The process of spiritual transformation through which our inner self is changed into the likeness of Christ involves the "renewing of the minds." It is hard work that requires new discipline, willingness, understanding, dedication, and most importantly, spiritual development. One does not suddenly start thinking and acting like Jesus, at least not all the time. It takes time and cooperative effort to really understand the message and teachings of Jesus.

Another related misconception within the Christian community might be about salvation, which is that by verbally accepting Jesus Christ as your Savior, and thinking about having faith, you are "saved." While it is true that one can't receive salvation by doing good deeds, you "don't get it" if you live in selfish disregard of others. Here is why: **Salvation** comes through realizing unity with Christ and your fellows. Believing in God means knowing that there is no spiritual separation between you and God, or between you and the rest of humanity. So, after pledging your "belief," you can live a life of habitual sin, but it will lead you away from salvation, because it is denial of what you say you believe in. Jesus was not shy about saying, "If after knowing the truth you choose to turn your back on it, to be lukewarm, or to be outright wicked as a lifestyle, I will not accept you as one of mine."

Perhaps yet another misconception is that when teaching fellow Christians, we need to sugarcoat things. Jesus did not sugarcoat. Truth: As the "Church," we should strive to be a spiritual training ground where we hear all of this. And there should be considerable emphasis placed on Prayer, what it is and its importance to the individual moving from surface Christianity towards transformation, and in effecting positive change in the world.

Many of us misunderstand existence or being, thinking of it as physical (matter). Some think we are not spiritual, and this is not true. Webster's *Dictionary* defines immaterial as "not consisting of matter, spiritual." **Spirit** (the Pneuma, Chi, quantum field, energy itself), then, is defined as the unchanging real essence of something. It does not deteriorate, and cannot be destroyed, damaged, or hurt. A thought born into your mind exists, and does not consist of matter.

Did you know the meaning of the word **Genius** is "attendant spirit of a person," "extraordinary intellectual power," or "guardian deity (angel)?"

Within the universe, the physical is used to express ideas (the spiritual). The study of subatomic physics shows us that behind all physical objects are Divine ideas, and the Bible is devoted to teaching us about the power of thought and how to relate to the operating principles of the universe, but our conscious often focuses on the "physical" rather than on what it aims to convey.

A common error is to suppose that when the Bible speaks of "heaven," "the holy place," or "the secret place of the most High," that that place is somewhere outside of yourself, probably up in the sky, when in fact it is your own consciousness that is being discussed.

Jesus repeatedly taught, "But **seek first the kingdom of God** and His righteousness, and all these things shall be added to you.," (Matthew 6:33), and when asked where one could find it, He responded, "The kingdom of God is within you." This is the foundation of His whole teaching.

Just as Salvation might mistakenly be thought of as an event, the day you are taken to heaven, so too is Salvation about your conscious mind. It starts with your personal realization that what Jesus taught us about the nature of God, the universe, and its operating principles, as well as about existence, is the absolute truth. This is "believing in His name." Believing then, removes the "deception" we were previously under, the altered reality of thinking that we are primarily physical beings. As we "work out salvation," we are really overcoming the sense of separation from our source (God).

I'm not suggesting at all that we don't leave our physical body and enter a different realm, the heavenly realm. I am confident that we do. Rather, what I am suggesting is that Jesus teaches us that we arrive at that place by changing our understanding and working out our Salvation. Enoch reached heaven once he arrived at a constant state of realizing God's presence in his conscious day-to-day reality, through nonstop prayer or conscious dialogue with God.

God, as He reveals Himself in the Bible, is not a person in the normal sense of the word, but is relational, and has all the qualities of personality except limitation. In relation, He represents Himself as three personas: God the Father, God the Son, and God the Holy Spirit. This is sometimes confusing for people when we try to apply logic. "How can God the Father and Jesus [the Son] both be God if they are distinct persons? The three are different aspects of one God. God manifest Himself as Jesus [the man] to model for "us" our correct relationship to God as sons and daughters. The Holy Spirit is God's (Jesus's) spirit which exists within us (when we receive it). Think about us, for example: we have a mind with thoughts, a voice that speaks, and a heart that pumps, which are distinct parts of "one" being. Same concept here.

God is love, and another thought would be that love cannot exist with just one person. You need an object of love to relate to, hence Father and Son. This might be difficult for some to grasp with all the narcissistic effort our society puts into loving oneself, but that's not actually love — we'll get into that later. What's truly amazing is that if we pay attention, we will see the perfect love and concepts of family and community that God is modeling for us through the Father, the Son and the Holy Spirit, each honoring and glorifying one another, working together and deferring to each other in total cooperation and obedience to each other.

Jesus as the physical representation of God came into the world to save us from living in deception (to expose Satan's lies), to tell us the truth about ourselves, about existence, and about His true nature, and to teach us how to live, how to love, and how to relate to creation and the Creator, thereby bringing us out of the darkness and into the light.

> …He is the exact representation or exact character of God. (Hebrews 1:12, New King James Version)
>
> …He is the image of the invisible God. …By Him all things were created that are in Heaven and that are on earth, visible and invisible, whether on thrones or dominions or principalities or power. All things were created through Him. (Col 1:15-16)
>
> …For this purpose the Son of God was manifested, that he might destroy the work of the devil. (1 John 3:8)
>
> … I and the Father are one. (John 10:30)
>
> … And His name is…everlasting Father. (Isaiah 9:6)
>
> … He who has seen Me has seen the Father. (John 14:9)

Jesus said in effect, "I'm God, you've got my words twisted, you've been deceived by the devil's lie about me. I'm not about domination through humiliation and violence, that's evil. I'm all about peace, love, and harmony… you're distorting Scripture to pervert my will… Let me tell you about yourselves, about existence, about me, and about love… Let me explain what we must contend with in living out love [resisting the temptation of deception] …I will teach you how to do this, and if you will believe in me (all that I'm telling you), and implement what I teach you, it will lead to heaven (the Kingdom where "we," humans, all of creation, and the Creator live in harmony).

Truth: Each of our lives, while distinct, is the same in that our total existence is about understanding the nature of God and relating to it. This can be extremely difficult since by and large we suffer from "contempt prior to investigation" and our two favorite words are "no," and "me." All joking aside, most of us have experienced longing, heartache, rejection, and abandonment. Too many have felt violence and hatred. If we are honest with ourselves, fear in one form or another (worry, anxiety, resentment, insecurity, anger, pride, selfishness, etc.) seems to be the primary driver of our thoughts and behaviors.

Truth: Depending on the extent to which we expand and extend our thoughts of God, we will find healing, love, acceptance, harmony, joy, and purpose in life. Stay with me as we think about it together. Not only will it make sense, but also, I promise you will get something good out of it!

Absolute Truth: There is a power available to transform you into your real self, to pick up from the midst of doubt, failure, ruin, misery, and despair; to heal your heartache, depression, addictions, and physical illness; and to deliver you safely on the road to happiness, freedom, and peace. All you need to do to have that Power start working in your life is to make conscious contact with Him. Again, He's not "out there somewhere;" rather, the connection to God dwells in your mental consciousness. I am not giving you metaphoric dialogue. This is absolute, literal, and practical truth.

4

THE LIE – A DISTORTED REALITY

"Oh what a tangled web we weave, when first we practice to deceive."

SIR WALTER SCOTT, "MARMION: A TALE OF FLODDEN FIELD"

One of the most important biblical concepts for us to grasp completely is "the lie" that the serpent whispered to Eve in the Garden of Eden story, and how it creates fear today, which drives us and distorts our systems of thought (society's views, television programming, laws, institutions and teachings). From there, the concepts of sin, trusting God, salvation, and all the other core teachings of the Bible will become clearer, and more meaningful in context.

Many people reading the Bible have breezed through the beginning of Genesis, and miss God explaining what we are, who we really are, and describing to us "the lie" and the identity crisis, so to speak, that Eve and Adam spawned for mankind in having the false realization of being separated from God. Man became self-conscious instead of God-conscious. If we did read it, it probably did not make sense.

Let's take a look at **Genesis 1-3** together: With an understanding of Hebrew grammar and correct prepositions in the ancient Middle East, scholars today know that **Genesis 1:26** states that God made us "as" His image, not "in" His image, as the traditional translation suggests. So, we are not something kind of like or resembling God but are **literally** the living images of God's Spirit on earth. We are meant to be vessels that express, reflect, and magnify God's Spirit. The Hebrew term translated into "likeness" comes from the root word meaning to magnify. We are not just creatures that have moral, intellectual, and ethical abilities, and when we become aware of this, we can operate (think and believe) as designed. We are meant to be light bulbs, and God is the electricity!

Genesis 2:15 says that God placed man into the protection of living softly, in a state of pleasure (the meaning of the words **Garden** and **Eden**). Then in **verse 2:17**, God provides the simple instruction to maintain this gentle and fulfilling life: man should not get involved in trying to figure out how to control things. He warns that in becoming consumed with obtaining personal power and self-sufficiency, man will break everything into pieces, spoiling his life. He says it will lead to death, spiritually and physically (the meaning of the **tree of knowledge of good and evil**).

What is being described in the book of Genesis when the serpent lies to Eve – be it literal or symbolic of man's state – is humankind's demise. We're not talking about the story we heard as children, in which Eve bites the apple.

In **Genesis 3:1**, the serpent tricks Eve by twisting the meaning of what God says. It literally says, "the whispered incantation put her under a spell." The lie told is that God can't be trusted. He wants to control and oppress Eve, and then in **verses 3:4-5**, that if Eve pursues personal power through acquiring knowledge and things, she will be in control of her life and will be self-reliant. In **3:6**, the woman perceives that these ideas are good, takes delight in them, longing to become secure, and focuses on attaining knowledge and getting or consuming attractive, desirable things.

Key word look-up: Here are the original ancient Hebrew terms and their meanings so you can see for yourself, using Strong's Exhaustive Concordance.

GENESIS 2:15			
English word	Original Hebrew	Meaning	Strong's #
Garden	gan from ganan	**fenced, protected (to hedge)**	1588
Eden	eden	**pleasure; from 'to be soft'**	5731

GENESIS 2:17			
Tree	ets	**to make firm (from its firmness/tree)**	6086
Knowledge	da'ath	**to know; from 'to ascertain by seeing'**	1847
Good	towb	**to be or make well (healthy, fortunate, prosperous)**	2896
Evil	ra	**adversity, affliction, calamity; from 'to spoil by breaking into pieces'; 'to render good for nothing'**	7451 &7489
Eat	akal	**to consume, burn up, devour**	398

GENESIS 3:1			
Serpent	nachash	**'to whisper an incantation' (an enchantment)**	5175/72&73
Subtle	aruwm	**cunning from smoothness**	6175
Beast	chay	**alive**	2416
Field	sadeh	**spread out**	7704
Eat	akal	**to consume, burn up, devour**	398
Tree	ets	**to make firm**	6086
Garden	gan	**protected**	1588

GENESIS 3:4-5			
Die	muwth	**die, cease**	4191
Eyes	'ayin	**focus, perspective**	5869

Opened		**'to be observant'**	6491
Knowing	d'ath	**to know, from 'to ascertain by seeing'**	
Good for food	tuwb + ma'akal	**good to consume**	2896/3978
Pleasant	ta'avah	**longing**	8378
Eyes	'ayin	**focus point, perspective**	5869
Tree	ets	**to make firm**	6086
Desired	chmad	**to delight in, covet, desire**	2530
Wise	sakal	**to be circumspect and intelligent**	7919
Fruit	periy	**to bring forth**	6529
Eat	akal	**to consume, burn up, devour**	398

Satan's lie to Eve was essentially that God could not be trusted, which meant Adam and Eve were on their own, left to fend for themselves. This belief that we can't trust God leads to notions of abandonment, unworthiness, separateness, self-reliance, and independence – man's self-consciousness, the awareness of me, creating fear (sin), which leads to selfishness.

This lie is so pervasive and effective that it is embedded in all of society today, and has even affected how we have read, interpreted, and taught the Bible over the course of time, encouraging false notions of God, and in turn false notions of self; the idea that God is either non-existent or a punishing killer, and the idea that we're either helpless, unworthy, or corrupt.

This belief then, **sin**, would of course be handed down to their children, and their children's children, and so on throughout mankind. In the world, we teach our children the notion of separateness, which is perpetuated throughout everything in society. This masterful spell of deception is a self-perpetuating lie that robs mankind of its true identity and diverts us from our created purpose.

Embedded in our notion of being separate, "the ego," is extreme fear and mistrust. Since we believe that we have to protect, guide, feed, and shelter ourselves, we feel compelled to try to control our circumstances and the environment around us to ensure that we'll be all right.

Sin: A common notion of sin is that it means doing something bad, something evil, an act that violates one of the ten commandments. The actual meaning of the word sin is the denial of the truth about God, that He exists and is trustworthy – the thought that you are separated from God and are something less than a spiritual being – and all the associated thoughts and actions that follow. In essence, it's participating in or being under the influence of **the lie** (that we can't trust God). The Greek word **harmartia,** from the words *hamartano* and *meros*, translated in the English speaking Bible as sin, means "to err" in thought, or "not to share" in the truth. The Hebrew word **chata,** translated as sin, means "to miss," to forfeit, or to lead astray.

Psychology acknowledges sin as a synonym for neurosis (the human condition) and describes it as the "denial of the miraculousness of our creation and existence," and as the repression of the truth of our identity, a lie.

Here's how I understand sin: Sin is the condition of unbelief, as fallen man, the denial that we are spiritual beings. It is the sense of separation from God; the belief that ultimately we are alone, have to provide for and protect ourselves and our children if we have them; that each of us alone has to shoulder the pressure of figuring out how to make life work and make the right critical decisions. And sin is all of the fearful, doubtful, anxiety-filled thoughts we have as a result of this – and all of the selfish, greedy, impulsive, mean, deceitful, violent, hurtful acts we engage in – out of desperation, panic, and perhaps the desire to overcome fear by self-medicating (retail therapy, food addictions, drugs, alcohol, sex, risk-taking etc.) In truth, **sin is fear**. To fear is to be in a state of not believing in or trusting God.

> *"There is no fear in love, but perfect love (which is God) casts out fear (which is unbelief and the ideas of Satan). For fear has to do with torment (punishment) and whoever fears has not been made perfect in love (God)."* –1 John 4:18.

- It really is not about being good or bad, it's about believing that "you are not alone," that God takes care of you, or believing "the lie that you are alone." All behavior falls out of these two camps of thought.

- None of us are inherently evil or corrupt, but humanity apart from God is no more capable of living selflessly than an addict is of recovering from an addiction by willpower.

> *"As it is written, None is righteous, no, not one, for all have sinned and fall short of the glory of God."* –Romans 3.

By the way, there are 16 different terms used in the original Hebrew and Greek Scriptures that English translation reduced to the word evil. Almost all of those terms are talking about "wrong thought," and the "hurtful and worthless things we say to injure each other," most frequently described as "coming from a place of mental anguish and emotional pain" or "the sense of being alone, unworthy of love," and "not enough" – specifically NOT from "being corrupt or foul at the core."

I don't know about you, but when I watched *The Wizard of Oz* as a child, no one explained that the Wicked Witch was a hurting, lonely woman who felt unworthy of love and who was under the influence of a lie (the meaning of the Hebrew word translated into **wickedness**). That's actually the tone and context that the Bible uses when teaching about "evil" and "wicked."

We ourselves distort their meaning, along with words like "condemnation" and "vanity."

Take **vanity,** for example. When we accept the accuser's lies, we think of a vain person in the context of being conceited about their appearance. In concrete terms, we think of a woman putting on makeup. We might label a vain person as "insecure" or ridicule them as shallow, as if they are messed up and less than others. The Bible's teachings on vanity have us looking with compassion at why there's a preoccupation with performance and acceptance. Why do people even need to wear makeup? The Merriam-Webster Dictionary defines vanity as "a thing that is empty or useless; the quality or fact of being useless or futile."

The Bible talks about how parents mistakenly teach shame and give their children the message that they must perform in order to be valued; that they must be more than just themselves in order to be accepted and loved. The girl whose parents believe "the lie" might then be taught shame and abandonment and live in fear of not being enough. She might try extremely hard to be a perfectionist, a good girl, a high performer, and she will surely try to conform to society's message that if her body is attractive, she will be accepted and wanted. In fact, she'll quickly figure out that sexual seduction gives her a sense of power to control being wanted by men. As she grows older, she may develop an eating disorder and dream of plastic surgery. Isn't it truly heartbreaking that someone would exert themselves to chase love and acceptance, or share what is meant to be the most intimate expression of two people embracing and loving each other as they are, for who they are, with numerous partners, and come up empty-handed, not finding validation, but instead taking on further shame?

The original ancient Hebrew and Greek terms used in the Bible describe vanity as:

- The idea of tentative manipulation; the unsuccessful search; without purpose.
- Exerting oneself only to arrive at naught.
- An attempt to rush over devastation.
- Self-punishment; "gnawing" at oneself.

The lie that you are not loved just as you are, that you are unwanted, unworthy, alone, unprotected, cut off, and abandoned, is just that, a total lie, told for the purpose of our destruction.

Note: The English word **angel** used in the Bible is in place of the ancient Hebrew term *malak* and the Greek term *aggelos*, meaning "to dispatch a message" or "messenger," and comes from a root word meaning an "announcement." Regardless of what notions you apply when thinking about the concept of a celestial angel, whether it resembles a man, an invisible spirit, a dream, or some form of epiphany or realization, the term angel refers to a mechanism by which God communicates thought and ideas to us. The word **Satan** is a generic term meaning "accuser." For our purposes, let us think of the serpent or Satan as the collection of ideas and beliefs that are in opposition to our true nature as Beings, attacks on our thoughts, lies about our identity. The Hebrew term translated into **serpent** [*nachash*] literally means "an enchantment," or "to put under a spell."

FEAR

Let's look at **fear** and how it works. Fear is the primary alarm in response to present danger. It's a built-in instinct for quick mobilization of the body for fight or flight, enabling us to respond to emergencies. It involves the natural response of anger, which last only 90 seconds. This is not an intellectual experience, but rather an instinctive one. We're not talking about fear in that sense. We are talking about mental fear, things we imagine, the clinical manifestation of fear, from mild worry to chronic anxiety. These are "false alarms;" they are not real, but made up. Some of us react to stressful or negative life events, whether they are perceived or real, in much the same way we do to physical threats, while others may be less affected. In either case, fear in all its forms (worry, resentment, pride, jealousy, lying, bragging, and seduction) are harmful. Professionals treating people for clinical anxiety, depression, PTSD, or panic attacks look at cognitive distortion (wrong beliefs) for which they offer therapy, and biological dysregulation (brain chemistry) for which they offer pills, but the root cause is twofold: separation anxiety, and the experience of stressful life events. Obviously, our thoughts, evaluations, interpretations, and appraisals of a situation or an event will define whether they are stressful. If they are projected, future, negative events that we worry about, then they are stressful. These false alarms trigger the same protection mechanisms and physiological effects as a real threat of imminent danger. We are designed to deal with imminent threats, things we can respond to and be done with, but the world we live in has us under constant attack. We have lots of unresolved worries and fears. Chronic fear and emotional pain cause depression, PTSD, and mood disorders, and depress the immune system, encouraging asthma, inflammatory and autoimmune disease, cancer, cardiovascular disease, and type 2 diabetes.

Another impact is that **fear interferes with our ability to think clearly**. The forebrain or conscious mind, which is the hub of reasoning and logic, is about a thousand times slower than the reflex action controlled by the subconscious, so we are designed to use the faster processing of the subconscious in emergency situations. <u>We are dumber when in a fearful state</u> because our conscious reasoning shuts down when the mind perceives a threat and the faster subconscious takes control. Our subconscious mind is where our beliefs and memories are stored. So, if we have false beliefs and they are tied to memories that we perceive as painful or scary, those are the "tapes" we will continually play, and the thoughts we will act on automatically (reflexively), when under stress. An example would be when someone you love verbally attacks you, and before you can stop yourself, you say something that you regret.

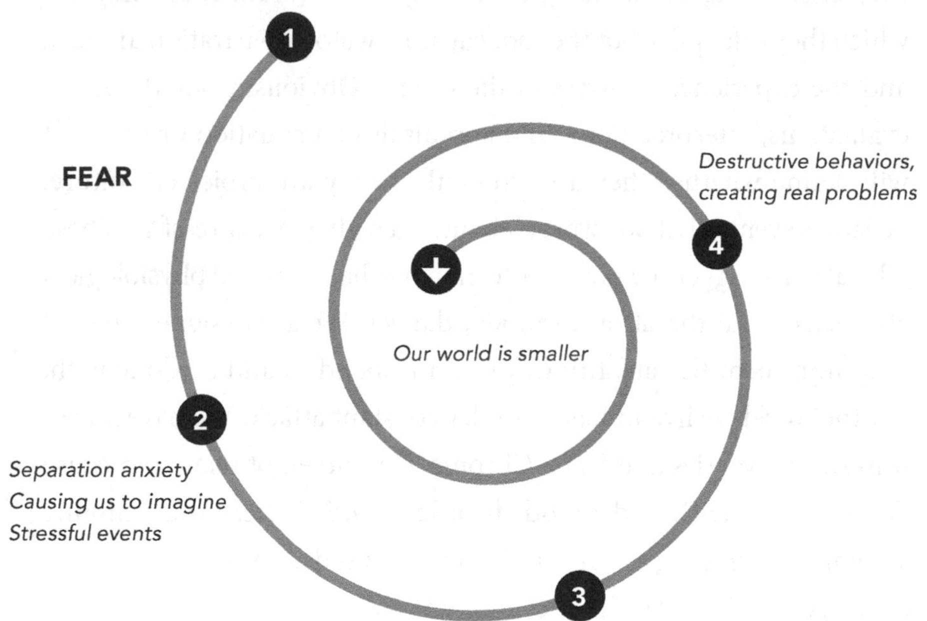

We become selfish because we want to control those "perceived" stresses (2). We try to control and manipulate people, situations, and circumstances; we are rude, selfish, we lie, we cheat, we are jealous, we are greedy. We want to be accepted, we want to be safe, and we long to be loved (3). Most of the imagined situations we worry about never come to fruition, but we create real, stressful relationship problems with our behaviors. Our world gets smaller and smaller. * This diagram can apply to a corporation, institution, or government, as well as to an individual. Once the spirit of fear is the influence behind a power, the cycle occurs.

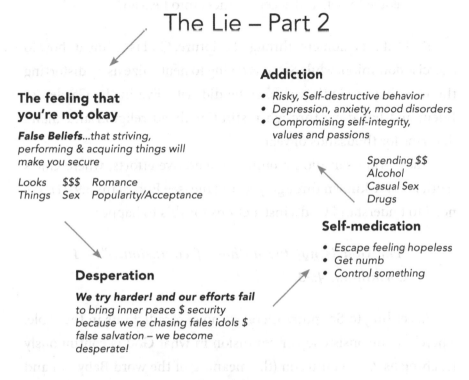

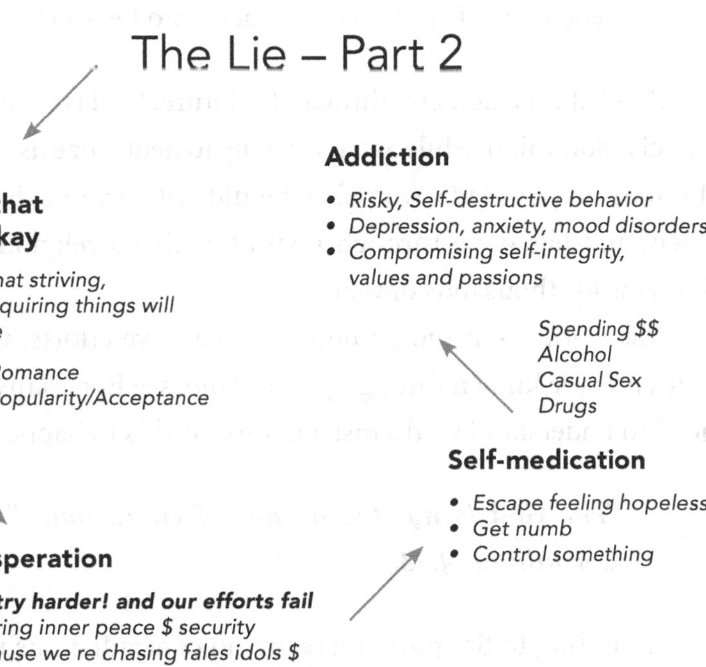
The Lie – Part 2
Addiction
• Risky, Self-destructive behavior
• Depression, anxiety, mood disorders
• Compromising self-integrity, values and passions
The feeling that you're not okay
False Beliefs...that striving, performing & acquiring things will make you secure
Looks $$$ Romance
Things Sex Popularity/Acceptance
Spending $$
Alcohol
Casual Sex
Drugs
Self-medication
• Escape feeling hopeless
• Get numb
• Control something
Desperation
We try harder! and our efforts fail to bring inner peace $ security because we re chasing fales idols $ false salvation – we become desperate!

Twisting the meaning of God's words...

When you read the Bible, do you have a clear understanding of what God is teaching you about yourself, as a being made to reflect and express His Spirit, or are you not sure? Do you feel like you get some of what you read in the Bible, but not everything? Do you see contradictions, for example?

- Jesus is the "only begotten son," but we're sons and daughters, too?
- There's no fear in love. God is love, but we should fear God?

- "God never changes," but instructed people to kill their enemies before Jesus was on earth, and then Jesus taught against killing, telling us to "love our enemies?"
- Jesus "reconciles **<u>all</u>** things into Himself," and yet sends some people to hell and accepts others into heaven?

Right at this moment, through Scripture, God is telling us how to exercise dominion, while Satan is trying to neutralize us by distorting the meaning of God's words, as he did with Eve in the Garden of Eden, and has done through institutionalized religion and man's doctrine for thousands of years.

The world's salvation requires cooperative efforts, where God's truth is made known through you and me (see Ephesians 3:9-11). We need to understand God's instructions for this to happen.

> ***"For God <u>is not</u> the author of confusion…" – 1 Corinthians 4:33.***

According to Scripture there are no contradictions in the Bible. There's no inconsistency or confusion in what God is continuously teaching us. Our confusion (the meaning of the word Babylon) and misunderstandings occur when we are manipulated into seeing what Satan wants us to see. God tells us to prove all things, while the enemy deceives us by getting us to accept things without questioning, according to 1 Thessalonians 5:21.

> *"And the great dragon was cast out, that old serpent, call the Devil and Satan which deceiveth the whole world…"* – Revelation 12:9.

Many of us read the Bible looking at the stories and people, rather than looking for the spiritual teaching.

> *"As a society we are in the habit of taking superficial glasses at things, not taking close looks, and we gauge things by worldly standards – not by spiritual standards" – 2 Corinthians 10:7 (author's translation)*

Exodus 32:26-29 is a great example of where merely reading the English translation makes God seem untrustworthy. It seems to describe a scene where Moses (on behalf of God) instructs Levites to kill non-believers or sinners…"Let every man slay his brother, every man his companion, and every man his neighbor...And about three thousand men of the people fell that day."

This Scripture does not actually talk about slaying people with swords in the way we might assume in reading it. It talks about a great day where many people were shown "the lie," put aside self-destruction, and received salvation. It's about mass salvation, not mass murder.

> Jesus explains, *"Truly, I say to you. If you have faith and do not doubt…what you ask in prayer, you will be given." – Matthew 12:119-22.*

How can you not doubt if you see contradictions in what the Bible says about who God is, about His nature? If you doubt, how can you be effective in prayer?

Here's a question: would you willingly entrust your life and your loved ones to the care of a leader whom you knew to be a ruthless, violent killer? Would you trust a leader who had power, but let bad things happen to people? For most of us, an honest answer is no, not so much. We might fear him, but we wouldn't trust him.

Assume for a moment that there truly is a spirit in opposition to truth, an accuser (Satan). Ambiguity, confusion, distortion, and manipulation of meaning would surely be in its primary tool kit (the manifestation of Babylon).

If you've ever read two opposing legal briefs, you would quickly see the opposing sides citing the same case law, but pretending it means the opposite of what the other side said. This is very effective in neutralizing. Satan is the prosecutor.

What do you hear when you read, "obey my will?" Does it sound controlling? If it does, we should ask why. It's because from ancient times on, our society has taught a false notion of God's nature. We take commands as forceful dominance coming from a great power. We assume the meaning of words through that lens.

Jesus very clearly taught that our notion of God was distorted. He specifically taught against domination, oppression, force, violence, selfishness, judgement, and exclusion. He taught love, selflessness, forgiveness, and nonviolence. He taught about free will, not force, and He stated He was gentle. Somehow, we believe anti-Christ teaching (the opposite of what He taught), even when we read the Bible.

Here's what God saying "obey my will" would mean in the Bible: "really listen to and believe my guidance." He never forces us. "Obey," or *shama* in Hebrew, means "to hear" and "to really listen to," and "will," or *thelema* in Greek, means "heart's desire for you." It's a Father urging or pleading with His child not to blow Him off, but to listen to His loving guidance.

Let me illustrate what I am talking about through a personal story. Consider this scenario: my father killed himself right before Christmas when I was nine. I was alone when I found him dead. He had a serious alcohol problem, and I don't think he could stop. One night when he was drunk, he was choking my mom. She was turning blue, so I tried to get him off her. Then he started choking me. It took two men to pull him off me. The next day, when he learned what he had done, he was crying and apologizing. I could tell he was mortified and distraught when he saw his handprints on my throat. When he wasn't drunk, things were good: he loved his family and we loved him. I prayed to God every day on my way home from school that my dad wouldn't drink, but God never answered my prayers. I've struggled with addiction and alcoholism, too, and been married and divorced three times. My life has always been filled with grief waiting in the background. Life's been a tease of "almosts." I was almost happy, almost successful. If we talk about God or the Bible, you'll hear hurt and anger in my tone. I cannot hide how unjust I think God is, this God that I say doesn't exist.

The denial of God because of hurt and anger is fairly common. "If God is all-powerful, and is love, I must not be worthy of love, or He's not loving," we think.

All of us have been hurt, some a whole lot, but what stops us from living our right life, from fulfilling our glorious purpose, is that most of us don't trust God, and as a result, we're afraid of not being loved, not being able to love, and for some, we're also afraid to be loved.

My dad was the nine-year-old boy who found his alcoholic father dead from a suicidal overdose in the trailer park. They lived in a trailer park because my grandfather lost his job and his family's home due to his alcoholism. My father is unwilling to take risks that involve getting his hopes up in an effort to control and minimize the emotional pain that he perceives the world will offer him if he interacts with it. We don't have much of a historical relationship because he didn't interact with me a lot when I was growing up. For the most part, I lived with my mother and sister.

Ten years before I had a child, I was reading books on being a father and the importance of that role. I promised myself that I would be a good, engaging, caring father, and yet I've been through multiple marriages. I have a completely different personality and outlook from my father, but I've repeated the generational cycle. I have lost jobs and homes, creating havoc and terror for my wives and children. I've been that engaged, caring father who then blows his children's lives apart because he can't deal with his emotions as they relate to rejection and perceived abandonment. Even after finding Christianity, becoming involved in ministry leadership, and feeling called to be a pastor, and even though I abstained from alcohol on a day-to-day basis, I still reverted to it when I hit a wall in my marriage. Back then, I didn't know it, but my identity and sense of being okay was wrapped up in the roles I fulfilled rather than in Christ.

What about not trusting God because of our notion of Him beyond our own hurts, from what we understand the Bible to indicate about God's nature? I was on a pay phone with my father while I was in jail, attempting to share my passion about some of the things I had become aware of in terms of teachings in the Bible that are frequently misunderstood. I'd spent many hours a day for the past two years passionately and intensely studying Scripture and developing a working relationship with Jesus. My father knew I had become a Christian years before, but this was the first time we had talked about faith. He was telling me how impressed he was with how I was handling all that had happened to me by way of betrayal and losing my liberty and the life I had (reputation, relationships, career, possessions). I was telling him I wouldn't give back the work that God had done in me, showing me truths and changing my false beliefs.

As we talked, he shared his fatherly concern that in studying the Old Testament, I would likely lose my faith. He asked, "how can you believe in the Jewish God of the Bible who is so violent and twisted that He instructs parents to have their sons murdered because of disobedience?" referred to the book of Deuteronomy. I told him I didn't know the passage he was talking about but was confident that it did not say what it seemed, so I would find out and get back to him. Of course, he had no interest in talking more about the Bible. In fact, he's cut our calls short in anger several times when I've brought it up.

Looking for some explanation, I called and e-mailed a few friends who were pastors. But all I got back was the standard response they were taught to use: "We don't know why God does what He does but...," referring to Deuteronomy 29:29.

I love how God works! In order to help my father see what I knew to be the true nature of God—loving, gentle, and trustworthy—I really had to learn how to study Scripture, looking up every original word used and its meaning. Being able to see the Spiritual teachings in the Bible clearly was the most amazing gift. I've learned how to become effective in prayer, and am truly smarter today because of my encounters with God through Scripture.

I love my father deeply. I feel for him and want him to have salvation, not just in the eternal sense, but right now, in this lifetime. I want him to experience Christ's love, and I pray that he will encounter Truth.

> *"If a man has a stubborn and rebellious child who will not obey the voice of his father and the voice of his mother, and who when they chasten him, will not heed them, then the father and the mother shall take hold of him and bring him out to the elders of his city, and shall say to the elders of his city, 'This son of ours is stubborn and rebellious, he will not obey our voice, he is a glutton and a drunkard. Then all the men of this city shall stone him to death with stones, so you shall put away the evil from among you, and all Israel shall hear and fear."* – Deuteronomy 21:18-21

The way most English-speaking people read it, this section of the Bible says a father and mother are instructed to take their misbehaving son to the elder men in their city to be stoned to death.

Sounds like a loving God, right? I know the teachings of Jesus, and I know that God is sovereign. He does not change. So when I first read this, I knew that what it seemed to be saying at face value had to be wrong (not the Scripture itself, but my understanding of it). It was "not possible" for God to have been ruthless, violent, and punishing before Christ on earth, and then to have had a change of heart, because God "never changes" (see Malachi 3:6). Jesus always told us and showed us that we had a distorted notion of His nature.

By the time I dove into this passage of Scripture to see what it said, I knew I wasn't looking for the concrete or physical situation (the problem statement), as much as the spiritual teaching (the root cause always being 'wrong thought,' and the solution always being to raise one's awareness by contemplating God, the Indwelling Spirit). Nonetheless, I was taken aback to see that most of my base assumptions about words' meaning, context, and even the description of the situation were false when I looked up the original Hebrew terms used.

When we decode the English translation, we see at a surface level a situation where a son is making a mess of his life. He is bitter and withdrawn, and won't listen to his parents' advice or instruction. He is morally loose and a drunkard. The instruction is to take him to the elders of the city, tell them what's going on, and have them "cast together support" to "begin again or rebuild" this young man and his life.

The story, which is the backdrop in English to demonstrating spiritual truths about how we as humans work, is suggesting that sometimes it takes a community to raise a child. It's about discipleship and men coming alongside a younger guy. This is vastly different from having the men of your city throw rocks at your son and kill him, because he's not obeying. **Stone** was used was the English word used in place of the ancient Hebrew term *ragam*, meaning "to cast together" and **stones**, translated from *eben*, was not a plural of that term, but means "to build up or rebuild." The spiritual teaching is about the lie of self-reliance, and how to "take your thoughts captive" and "renew your mind." The son is your identity. The father symbolizes the chief idea. And the mother represents the bond of your identity to the chief idea. The city is your consciousness, the reality you see. The elders are those mature spiritual ideas, your knowledge of truth.

You are instructed to go to those ideas, and they will cast together the collection of thoughts needed to replace and repair your fear: rebellious, backsliding, arrogant, negative thoughts, so that you will stop creating adversity, affliction, drama, and chaos in your life – and your identity will be in God. That's what the original ancient Hebrew scripture actually says.

Read the original terms used and their meaning:

English word	Original term	Meaning
man	*iysh*	to be, exist (individual, idea, thought)
stubborn	*carar*	to turn away
rebellious	*marah*	to be bitter
child (son)	*ben*	builder of family name; identity
obey	*shama*	to hear (intelligently)
voice	*qowl*	to spark peace
father	*ab*	principal; chief (idea)
mother	*en*	bond of family
chastened	*yacar*	to instruct
heed	*shama*	to hear (intelligently)
then	*arown*	to pluck; the act of gathering up
take	*laqach*	to seize; to carry away
elders	*zaqen*	mature
gate	*sha'ar*	an opening
his city	*ayar*	through the idea of opening the eyes, one's awareness or consciousness

glutton	*zalal*	shake, quake (unstable)
drunkard	*cobe*	to be full of self
stone	*ragam*	to cast together
death	*muwth*	to cease
stones	*eben*	to build up; to rebuild (identity)
evil	*ra*	adversity, calamity, affliction
Israel	*yisrael*	the idea that God will rule
hear	*shama*	to hear (intelligently)
fear	*yare*	to revere, to be in awe of

Deuteronomy 29:29, the verse that pastors often refer to when they have no answer about something in the Bible that seems like a contradiction, actually does not say, "we don't know why God does what He does..." It says that "topics not revealed to us belong to God, but those topics or matters (the Hebrew term *dabar*) that we become aware of are ours and our children's to solve...so that we can understand and then follow God's instructions." In other words, **when you see a contradiction in something said in the Bible, you should study to resolve it**. We have an obligation to exercise the minds He gave us.

There are many examples of this same teaching on overcoming "the lie" (fear) throughout the Bible. Here are a few.

EXAMPLE: DANIEL 6 – HOW TO OVERCOME FEAR

The story of Daniel's faith, which brought him out of a pit of lions unharmed, is exactly the teaching on how to overcome fear and trouble by correctly applying the law of dominion that we have as an expression of God's Spirit. As it is typically understood, it is also the epitome of spiritual teaching getting lost in translation. The original Hebrew writing makes the spiritual teaching of overcoming Satan's lie exceptionally clear, as it does the connection to the physical circumstance.

Daniel represents every person, and the scenario represents the human experience in general. When a problem comes into our lives, or fear into our thoughts, we are thrown into a pit of lions, so to speak. The Bible tells us that every individual difficulty we face is an occurrence on some scale of believing in "the lie." Outer conditions don't have power in and of themselves, but when we don't know that, or we forget, we fall prey, buying into ideas of limitation (the world's view, anti-Christ teaching).

The solution to overcoming any problem is always the same: to focus our thoughts on the Truth, that the Spirit of God is within us. As we know that God has no limitations, there's no condition that He can't produce, no circumstance He can't change, and there is no fear in God. Quite literally, the key to being physically unharmed by wild animals is not fearing them. Ask anyone who works with them.

The story opens with Daniel, one of three governors under King Nebuchadnezzar, impressing the new ruler Darius. When Darius contemplates promoting Daniel above the other governors, they plot to discredit him. The governors devise a plan to get him charged with a crime, forcing Darius to publicly punish Daniel. They can't find fault with Daniel, so they use his loyalty in praying to his God. The governors establish a royal statute decreeing that anyone who petitions any god or man other than Darius during a 30-day celebration shall be cast into a pit of lions.

Verse 10 says, **"Now when Daniel knew that the writing was signed, he went home. And in his upper room, with his windows open towards Jerusalem, he knelt down on his knees three times that day, and prayed and gave thanks before his God, as was his custom since early days."** Daniel was found praying, and was thrown into a pit of lions, which was then sealed shut. The king checked on Daniel the next morning, and Daniel was unharmed. In Verse 22, Daniel says, **"My God sent his angel and shut the lions' mouths,**

so that they have not hurt me, because I was found innocent before Him…"

What we get when we simply read the English translation is something like, Daniel went home and prayed, opening his windows towards the west (Jerusalem was to his west), and then because Daniel was found innocent before God and was faithful and innocent, he was saved. This type of interpretation is kind of on track about what physically occurred in the story, but misses the spiritual teaching completely.

The Hebrew Scripture actually says that Daniel understood the principles God taught, kept those teachings fresh in his mind, and turned inward with his thoughts towards the Indwelling Spirit in prayer during times of fear and trouble. He correctly applied the law of our Being and the law of dominion, demonstrating faith (see Hebrews 11:1).

In studying these verses by simply looking up all the words in the concordance and learning their meaning, they would read like this:

Verse 10: **"Now Daniel knew the writing was signed and** (*aial*) **thrust himself** (*bayith*) **inward, to the place within. And in his** (*allyth*) **highest level of thought, with eagerness and intense mental application** (*kav*)**, opened wide the gate to understanding, toward** (Jerusalem) **the teaching founded in peace. He knelt down three times that day and** (*bah*) **applied the principle taught, contemplating the Indwelling Spirit of God and His supremeness, delivering praise and thanks, as was his custom since early days."**

Verse 22: **"My** (*elahh*) **Almighty strength God** (*shlach*)**, misled** (*malak*) **a dispatched message to** (*cegar*) **shut up** (*pum*) **the talk, the voices of the** (*aryeh*) **gathered violent young thoughts** (what modern psychologists call a 'complex')**, so that they have not** (*ehabal*) **bound, tightly wound, perverted, or ruined me, because** (*shkach*) **through the idea of disclosure, I was found not to be oblivious, I had not mislaid the truth, but was clear or pure in thought."**

KEYWORD LOOKUP

The Hebrew words in parentheses above are the **specific** terms used in the Scripture as originally written. I looked up every word in the passage in the *Strong's Exhaustive Concordance*, and only noted those terms whose meaning is different from what we might commonly assume in reading the English word.

Angel [*malak*] #4398
Room/Chamber [*alliyth*] #5952
God [*elahh* from *elowahh* and *el*] #s 426/433/410
Found [*shkach* from *shakeach*] #
House [*haggish*] #4398
Hurt [*ehabal*] #2255
Innocent/Innocency [*zakuw*] #2136
Jerusalem [*Yeruwashalem*] #3390
Lions [*aryeh* from *ariy*] #s 744/717
Mouths [*pwn* from *peh*] #s 6433/6310/6317
Open [*pethreh*] #6606
Praying [*bah, benh*] #1156
Sent [*shlach*] #7972
Shut [*regar*] #5463
Window [*kav* from root word *lahey*] #s 3551/3854

Literally, the Hebrew rendering would read more like this:

Verse 10: **"Now Daniel knew the writing was signed and (*aial*) TRUST HIMSELF (*bayith*) INWARD, TO THE PLACE WITHIN. And in his (*alliyth*) HIGHEST LEVEL OF THOUGHT with (*kav*, from the root word *lahag*) PIERCING EAGERNESS, INTENSE MENTAL APPLICATION (*petach*), opened wide the gate to understanding TOWARD (*yeruwasalem*). THE TEACHING FOUNDED IN PEACE, he knelt down three times that day (*bah/***

beah) **CONTEMPLATING THE INDWELLING SPIRIT OF GOD AND HIS SUPREMENESS** (applying the principles taught), **delivering praise and thanks, as was his custom since early days."**

We can learn a lot from Daniel. He correctly turned his thoughts to the realization of God in prayer three times a day as a way of life. In reading the entire book of Daniel, one can see that what made him effective in prayer was his study of scripture. He learned the laws taught (our operating instructions, cause, and effect) and applied those principles correctly in prayer. When he faced trouble, he didn't struggle to make contact with God, nor was he frozen in fear: he knew exactly what to do. He had "faith," and he knew from past demonstrations or evidence that applying the principles of our God, our instructions, would work!

We see the proof that outer conditions, even those with potential physical harm, are in fact influenced by our thoughts. We "actually" have dominion over animals or beasts on earth "if" we follow God's instructions. Daniel gave fear no power, hence the lions just hung out with him rather than attacking him.

THE LORD IS MY SHEPHERD — PSALM 23

This classic prayer is a treatment sent from God, for overcoming worry and anxiety. It should be read as a meditation. Read it through several times, pausing on each statement and realizing what it means. *If you were praying this for a group, it would be "our" and "we." I purposefully used "I" in the quotations so that you will claim these things for yourself as you read it. Oh yeah, and believing is a requirement.

1. The Lord is my Shepherd,
   A shepherd takes care of his sheep, and the Lord will take care of me because I am seeking Him now through this meditation.

I shall not want.

I have the knowledge that God is present in me. I only have to "realize" this truth, and everything negative in my life will vanish.

2. He makes me lie down in green pastures,

   Green pastures symbolize an abundance of the things I need; perfect harmony in my life.

3. He restores my soul, He leads me in the paths of righteousness

   He brings me back to right thinking.

   For His namesake.

   His all-powerful nature of goodness and love is taking care of me now.

4. Yea though I walk through the valley of the shadow of death,

   "Shadow of death" is my false belief, there is no death, only the sense that I've lost God's presence.

   I will fear no evil,

   I will not be afraid anymore; that's just "wrong thought."

   For You are with me.

   There's nothing to fear; Christ's Spirit is within me.

   Your rod and staff, they comfort me.

   This meditation has the power to bind, it is working right now.

5. You prepare a table before me in the presence of my enemies,

   The table, meaning a meal of spiritual teaching, and my enemies are my own fearful thoughts, doubts, self-criticism, and criticism of others.

6. You anoint my head with oil,

As I consecrate myself to You, Jesus, by meditating this way, I feel your response of gladness, praise, and thanks.

7. My cup runs over.
   I have complete assurance of the fullness of my rescue. I have a clear and total solution to my problems and their unseen causes.

God manifests Himself as a man to teach humanity about ourselves, existence, and His nature. As the prototype for true humanity, He models everything for us.

Living as a human, Jesus experienced life as we do. He felt love, but He also went through rejection, betrayal, hunger, thirst, anger, temptation, injustice, and extreme pain at the hands of His fellows.

As a man, He received the Holy Spirit when He consecrated Himself to the Father's mission, **as we are to do**. He demonstrated true love in acceptance of all who came to Him by working miracles to feed and heal, and never rejecting anyone who asked for help. He did it through prayer with "absolute" belief and faith, **as we are to do**. He wasn't just showing us how magnificent God is, He was showing us what to do! He was saying, this is how we do it, this is who we are, this is what our family stands for…"this is how you love," "this is how you awaken your brothers and sisters to the thought of spiritual existence and Me," and "this is how you pray to bring harmony to the world."

Truly, Jesus expected you and me to do the things He did. Jesus said, "most assuredly I say to you, he who believes in Me [not just in my existence, but that all I say is truth], the works that I do, he will do also, greater works than these he will do, because I go back the Father [back to that role]. And whatever you ask in My name, that I will do …" –John 14:12-14.

He didn't just expect that we "could" do the things He did, He expected that we would do them! "He gave them the power over unclean spirits, to cast them out, and to heal all kinds of sickness, and all kinds of disease...preach, saying, 'The kingdom of God is at hand.' Heal the sick, cleanse the lepers, raise the dead, cast out demons..." – see Matthew 10:1 8. Jesus said these were the signs that would follow those who believe (Mark 16:17). He didn't just expect that we would, but said that we didn't love Him unless we did these things; "He who has My commandments [understands them] and keeps them, it is he who love Me. And I will love him and manifest Myself to him" (John 14:21).

Satan doesn't want us to study and understand the instructions God provides for overcoming the lie, he wants us to be confused, and to have doubt, to be caught up in fear. If we're busy being worried about our lives, chasing money and pretty things, we are too distracted to learn, much less follow His instructions. Satan's goal is to neutralize our effectiveness, to make us vessels filled with fear, and unavailable to serve as a channel for God to live through.

EXAMPLE: ISAIAH 35:3-4

"Strengthen the weak hands, and make the feeble knees say to those who are fearful-hearted, be strong, do not fear! Behold your God will come with vengeance, with recompense of God: He will come and save you."

A COMMON interpretation from a Bible-literate person might be somethings like... "we can reassure ourselves with the knowledge that Savior is coming; we should tell fearful people to be strong, and not to fear...don't worry, it's alright, you are saved."

The SPIRITUAL interpretation, what the Author meant to

communicate, is a call to action...we are to pray with confidence until we see results. We are to pray expectantly.

Without awareness of the symbolism of hands throughout the Bible, we miss what Isaiah was passing along. Hands stand for the power to express God's ideas, to get results through prayer, to manifest God's will into the physical world.

The Latin word for hand (*manus*), was derived from the Sanskrit word meaning "thinker". That's where the English word for man came from. The Hebrew word in the Bible translated into "hand" is *yad*. It means the "power to express." The expression, "sit at the right hand of God", that is Christ's nature that manifests God through man. * We'll get into this in detail when we look at the meaning of Jesus's name, and the Spiritual Idea of the Son in the next chapter. This is how Isaiah 35:3-4 reads in the original Hebrew terms used. I inverted the English words in parentheses along with the Strong's Concordance reference # for ease of lookup.

"TIGHTEN UP (strengthen-2388) THE SLACK (weak-7504) IN YOUR POWER TO MANIFEST GOD'S IDEAS (hands-3027), AND BECOME ALERT OF YOUR WAVERING (feeble-3782) EFFORTS TO PRAY, (knees-1290) RESPOND (say-559) TO THOSE THOUGHTS THAT DO NOT HAVE A SOLID FOUNDATION, BUT ARE RASH AND TRANSIENT AT THEIR CORE, SAYING BE COURAGEOUS, do not be afraid! Behold, the GOD WITHIN YOU (God-430) CONSENTS TO COME (Will-14) WITH TREATMENT (recompense-1576) THAT VINDICATES (vengeance-5369). He will come and FREE (save-3467) you.

5

THE BIBLE ITSELF – BEYOND THE MISCONCEPTIONS

Most people have a general idea of what the Bible is and what it might contain, but in truth, one can't begin to understand just how vague or misleading that idea is until they "interact" with the Scripture contained in the Bible. By interacting, I mean using it like it tells us to, "read, study, contemplate and ask for understanding, then apply the principles it teaches to produce evidence of its truth."

People get caught up in trying to rationalize and minimize the Bible as a "book," with a "no thanks, we're good" attitude. I mean, what sane person surrenders their life's direction to the authority of a book? A book written, no less, by a bunch of different authors thousands of years ago in the Middle East, and not in our native language. Why would those men and women authors know anything about what would be good for us? We are self-sufficient, we are independent, and able to direct our own lives. We are not weak, mindless people who need instructions to follow. We do not need lots of rules to confine us! Each of us is capable of deciding what we want, what's best for us. We don't need "moral" teaching anyway, as long as we follow our nation's laws, we're fine. Besides, who says the Bible is the right guidance anyway? Look at the centuries of hypocrisy in the name of "Christianity."

We'll come back to address the "hypocrisy" a bit later, but first let's be honest about the "no thanks, we're good," attitude. The world is a mess. America, my country of origin, is no longer viewed by the international community as a great, compassionate, and just nation. Many of us don't even believe that ourselves.

Before getting into a discussion of what the Bible is and what it contains, I want to take a minute to talk about its importance to all U.S. citizens, regardless of their feelings about organized religion.

I have been wondering... did we ever consciously decide to stop handing down wisdom from generation to generation, or did it just happen? Did we determine that wise men, our elders and grandparents had nothing to offer and should be ignored or put away? A family name used to mean something; values, wisdom, and a code for living used to be taught and carried from generation to generation. It seems to me that in America, this ceased along with the teaching of anything biblical in schools (the wisdom of Proverbs, the prayer of Psalms, and the parables and teachings of Jesus).

- 1962 - Prayer in school became illegal (Engel v. Vitale)
- 1963 - Bible reading outlawed at school (Abington School District v. Schempp)
- 1980 - Posting of the Ten Commandments at school is against the law (Stone v. Graham)

We can look at our youth and see a media-based consumer society that spends more hours "plugged-in" than sleeping (studies show an average of thirteen hours a day), and try to impart blame on television and videogames, or now, social media and smartphones, but their existence in and of itself is not the problem. Certainly, reducing the time spent plugged in or online would be wise, but the real problem is "what" we watch or listen to in media land. If we watch shows that glamorize adultery and divorce, we might start to normalize those behaviors in our thoughts, and may start to think that strong, independent, liberated adults behave that way. We might feel entitled to branch out when bored or discontented with our marriage. I remember a study done eight years ago that showed three out of ten divorces were directly caused by cheating that started out as "innocent" flirting on Facebook and social media sites, and that was before smartphones and Facebook were in every household. If you watch killing glamorized, you'll likely normalize violence, especially if you think there is a "just cause." Just this week, there was an article/advertisement in *USA Today* talking up the new TV series *Lucifer*, which is all about glamorizing Satan.

I took an extension course at Harvard University on Constitutional History that really opened my eyes to the framework on which America was founded. The idea was to create a society where members were protected from government persecution and all people were treated as equals; where the governing bylaws and structure would create and enforce equality, liberty, and justice, things the founders believed were "God-given rights." America was founded on spiritual (Biblical) principles. Today, I seriously doubt that many people are really aware of this or know that understanding and living by those guiding principles is a critical success factor for the nation, its people, and our influence on the rest of humanity. My hope is that after rediscovering this, we collectively will care.

The founders of America were not Christian fundamentalists, but rather, intelligent spiritual men who believed in God, in the teachings of Christ, and in Biblical principles, just not in what the "church" had become. It was not the content of the Bible that they thought was wrong, but the Roman Catholic and English Christian churches. It was fallen leaders who twisted the words of scripture to fit their personal, sinful desire for power, making "Christianity" a loaded or contentious word.

"American values" of old, what made America a great nation, what inspired the founders to create a government for the people, by the people, were the spiritual teachings captured in the Bible. "Religious freedom" was meant to be freedom to worship God in the way that fits you, but it was never intended to mean freedom from religion, or freedom to remove God and our nation's guiding spiritual (Biblical) principles from our code of living right lives.

The intent was to create a "new age order" and "unfallen nation," one guided by the righteousness and spirituality of God. In fact, the success or failure of this new nation would depend on the adherence of its people to the country's spiritual values and framework. It would depend on Godly people and brotherly love.

With freedom comes responsibility to participate and contribute. The new nation welcomed people who wanted to participate in this society regardless of their country of origin, but they were expected and required to "join" it. America did not say, "Come all and start your own little countries here." It said come join us in a responsible, just, and decent community of brotherly love. Freedom to "do whatever I want" is exactly the selfish, sinful attitude that the founders of America were fleeing from. They were going for an attitude of people putting the welfare of the whole before their individual wants.

Unfortunately, most of us do not think about the great mission statement of our nation or its bylaws. I imagine that most people couldn't talk about the U.S. Constitution in any detail or identify its amendments. Many of us would not know that it is unconstitutional for an amendment to take rights away. The Constitution can only be amended to add liberty in order to ensure equal rights. Many would not know the Bill of Rights, nor have read the Declaration of Independence, and as such, would not be aware that God is throughout them. To those born in America, the principles used to be taught in school, and for those who gain citizenship through immigration, these principles are supposed to be learned and pledged: "I pledge allegiance to the flag of the United States of America, and to the republic for which it stands, one nation under God (dependent on God), indivisible, with liberty and justice for all." Government officials have to place their hand on the Bible to be sworn into office. People testifying in court used to be required to do the same, reminding us to place our trust in God and to be honest. Think about it, our currency says, "In God We Trust," and there is a depiction of the "Divine" all-seeing eye with the phrase NOUVUS ORDO SECLORUM (New Age Order), which according to Vladimu Rus, Ph.D. and expert in Latin to English translation and the meaning of symbols, is a reference to the "realities of this world as distinguished from the divine realities." Above the eye, it says, ANNUIT COEPTIS, meaning "He [God] is the divinity looking favorably on the new, but incomplete nation." E PLURIBUS UNUM, "Out of many, One," — We are members of the body of Christ, all connected together to God. One of our country's songs is *God Bless America*." Since the first session of Congress in April 1879, the U.S. Senate has opened in prayer, with our highest legislative body asking God to guide us. The founding documents of the nation say, "All men are endowed by their 'Creator' with certain unalienable rights." By "Creator" they were referring to God, not biological parents.

The intent of this nation was for its people to live out the godly ideas of liberty and the pursuit of happiness and justice by protecting its people from persecution and fostering compassion and brotherly love. The "American Dream" was about aspiring to fundamental decency, honesty, righteousness, morality, goodness, and brotherly love over self. Today, it seems like the American Dream is about entitlement to second homes, switching spouses when bored, quitting on families and friends when things get difficult, pursuing the excessive accumulation of wealth and material goods, and trying to get as many Facebook "likes" as our silently hurting "Selfies" can.

As the "freedom nation," we imprison more citizens than almost any other country, and are second in the world for the most laws. Think about that: with all of the notorious countries out there that are associated with inhumane policies and lack of civil rights, America imprisons a higher percentage of its citizens than most of them put together. America also has the highest divorce rate the biggest alcohol and drug problem of any country. And it goes almost unnoticed that fifty million people in our country don't have enough food to eat each year.

We lack commitment and faith. If we were honest with each other, we would admit that we lack hope for future generations. Sadly, to a large degree, we are a nation of self-focused consumers who look the other way to avoid being accountable to those in need. We are evil-doers. The international community no longer views the United States as the great compassionate and just nation. Many of us don't even believe this ourselves. Our nation is financially, morally, and spiritually bankrupt.

> "Politics is about people, and you cannot separate people from their spiritual values." —Daw Aung San Suu Kyi

Now might be a great time to look at and get back to the guiding principles, wisdom, and spirituality that our great nation was founded on, helping us to have the right spirits and powers behind our institutions, politics, and actions. I love what our country stands for on paper and has stood for by our actions many decades ago, make no mistake about it. However, we are a fallen nation, but we can be redeemed if we change our ways. "We can" practice Godly principles in all our affairs, as individuals and as a nation, but first, we have to be open to learning them. First, we have to be open to picking up a Bible and asking God to reveal truth to us.

> *"If my people who are called in my name will humble themselves, and pray and seek My face, and turn from their ways, then I will hear them from heaven, and I will forgive their sin and heal their land." (2 Chronicles 7:14).*

That does not mean imposing manmade laws or religious traditions that restrict free will. It does not mean that all Christians have to vote the same or that those who do not worship God via participation in organized religion cannot live right lives. In fact, it does not even mean that one has to be "Christian." However, if we want our nation to be successful, citizenship does require that one pledges to live out the Godly principles which are America's guidelines to spiritual progress.

I will use Alcoholics Anonymous as an example. Here is a successful society that practices freedom, but whose guiding principles are based on the Bible. AA members are a mixture of people, some who identify as non-religious, some who say they are spiritual, some ex-Catholic, Buddhist, Hindu, Muslim, and Christian. Free will is key, no one is forced to believe in a specific religion or concept of God, but by the same token, the entire program is based on accepting that there is a Higher Power (God), that as individuals we are powerless (against spiritual warfare) that He will restore us if we let Him (casting out the demon of alcohol and granting us Salvation; steps 1 & 2), then living out the Biblical principles of turning our will and lives over to the care of God (step 3), confessing our sins, accepting God's forgiveness and asking for our own (steps 4 & 5), truly repenting (steps 6, 7 & 8), and humbly asking forgiveness from others (9 & 10), and then working to improve conscious contact with God through prayer and meditation, seeking His will in all situations and the power to carry it out (step 11), and lastly, sharing the message with others and being of service (sharing the gospel of Salvation and loving your neighbors; step 12).

The sum total of someone practicing AA's principles in all of their affairs is a person who is living a God-centered life, someone who is working out their Salvation. Those that follow the "twelve steps" as a framework for living become honest, trustworthy, fair, dependable, responsible, loving, unselfish people who experience inner peace and joy. They start to overcome the sense of separation from God.

Interestingly, almost all people truly living by this framework receive miraculous blessings. The families, friends, jobs, and homes lost or destroyed through their sins are restored or replaced. Any sober recovering member of AA can tell you about the countless miracles that their Higher Power (God) has worked in their lives, amazing stories about wonderful things happening for them that are seemingly otherwise impossible.

We "**all**" need to recover from our fallen, fearful, selfish state; we all need to be restored. Perhaps the world could do well in applying the "twelve steps" generically (the Bible for dummies, so to speak). Maybe we should start holding one-hour meetings for everyone in society as daily schooling on how to live right lives.

The reason AA has continued to have success helping millions of people is because it allows for religious freedom without compromising or modifying its guiding principles. AA has not changed its texts because some are uncomfortable with the word God. "God" is used throughout AA, as is prayer. Most AA meetings open with the prayer that Jesus taught in Matthew 6:9-13, or the Serenity Prayer," which was written by an early Christian theologian. On page 99 of the "Twelve Steps and Twelve Traditions" is the prayer of Saint Francis as an example of the attitude one should cultivate in working on the 11th step, i.e. constantly praying to God. So we can see that "religious freedom" doesn't preclude a society from following Biblical principles, and that the U.S. was intended to do just that.

As it related to the hypocrisy of many claiming to be "Christians," we can rest assured that those were not people following the teachings of Christ captured in the Bible, but rather people who self-identified as "Catholic" or Christian without understanding the Truth and "the lie," or who chose to trade "the truth of God for the lie" in pursuit of personal power. We must not let the fact that 300 years after Christ, the Holy Roman Empire crucified Jesus, His Apostles and every Christian they could find, assimilated Christianity, and wrote their own doctrine telling us how to interpret the Bible rob us of the gift that is contained in scripture.

The Church(es) attached to empires and kingdoms surely perverted, distorted and mistaught scripture's meaning in order to support their organization as a power between man and God, but it is painfully obvious that they were not people following the teachings of Jesus, as they killed, persecuted, dominated, and oppressed people, the very things Christ taught against,

> "teaching as doctrine the commandments of men," and "making the word of God void in favor of their traditions." (Matthew 15:1-9).

Regardless of what foul men have taught, **I assure you that scripture itself, as written in the original manuscripts, is pure and free from error.**

To the priests Jesus said, "Why do you also transgress the

Commandment of God because of your tradition...? Thus you have made the Commandment of God of no effect by your tradition. Hypocrites! Well did Isaiah prophesy about you, saying, 'These people draw near Me with their mouth, And honor Me with their lips, But their heart (mind) is far from Me. And in vain they worship Me, Teaching as doctrines the commandments of men."

"...just as there will be false teachers among you, who will secretly bring in destructive heresies, even denying the Master (Jesus) who brought them... And many will follow their sensuality, and because of them the way of truth will be blasphemed. And in their greed they will exploit you with false words. (2 Peter 1-4).

"For certain men have crept in unnoticed, who long ago were marked out for their condemnation, ungodly men, who turn the grace of our God into lewdness and deny the only Lord God and our Lord Jesus Christ. (Jude 4).

Paul cautions us: "But I fear, lest somehow as the serpent deceived Eve by his craftiness, so your minds may be corrupted from the simplicity that is Christ. For if he who comes preaches another Jesus or different gospel which you have not accepted — you may well put up with it!" (2 Corinthians 11:3-4).

"I marvel that you are turning away so soon from Him (Jesus) Who called you in the grace of Christ, to a different gospel interpretation of Jesus (marriage), ...But there are some who trouble you and want to pervert the Gospel of Christ." (Galatians 1:6-7).

Jesus's doctrine was a new teaching (Mark 1:27). He wasn't just giving better versions of sermons taught about the Old Testament "law" in the Jewish temples. He wasn't attempting to put new wine in old wineskins (Mark 2:21-22). He absolutely was not teaching about replacing one oppressive power (Roman Empire) with another one (Roman Empire and Catholic Church).

He was correcting false teaching about the nature of God as

violent, exposing the world's systems and powers as under the deception of evil, and preaching peace, love, and the reconciliation of "all things."

On another track, there's much resistance to the idea that the scripture contained in the Bible is the "divinely inspired Word of God." First of all, does that suggest that God was literally controlling each writer's pen or that they were overtaken by the Holy Spirit? Does it mean that every single word chosen was God's choice, or that the writer was inspired with the core message, but exercised free will in how to express it? Then, since it wasn't the writers who selected which bodies of scripture made it into the Bible, but rather a series of councils hundreds of years later, are we to assume that they, too, were each inspired by the Holy Spirit in their selection?

Christianity has a bad name because men have lied about the meaning of scriptures in order to meet their evil, selfish needs. And I think we need to be quick to dispel anti-Christ behavior as being Christian, lest we follow the devil.

We could review several pages making a case with lots of data for the validity of the Bible (which I do in another book), but we won't. Instead, I will say this: from both personal experience and intense study, it would be a miracle if a person could construct the authoring of just one of the Bible's 66 books — which conveys specific messages, often to both the conscious and subconscious mind at the same time using direct writing, as well as poetry and a combination of ancient Middle Eastern symbolism and its own unique idioms, and have it be relevant over thousands of years to people with varied views on life, different levels of literacy and intellect, different social and economic positions, in different countries, who speak different languages, and who are all at different levels of spiritual development — and have its words meet each person right where they are on how to apply the general message to their specific life situation at that moment. Now this amazing miracle would need to be repeated with 40 different authors over 1,500 years in different cultures and countries. And it has, one way or another.

We could go through years of psychoanalysis and not scratch the surface of what the authors of Genesis, Isaiah and John, for example, knew about the subconscious mind and the way it functions. They knew what modern psychologists know today, and understood human nature as no other teachers have understood it. They knew all about what we call complexes and neuroses, cognitive distortion, the unconscious motive, phenomena of dissociation, splitting, etc. The plain fact is that the Bible is teaching man the absolute truth about ourselves, and we are foolish to ignore it.

From a rational and analytical perspective, people are always trying to compare, contrast, and group things in order to feel comfortable. However, there truly is nothing we can successfully compare the Bible to. It is not just a religious book and it is not "rational." It is miraculous and contains the voice and Word of God, which literally comes to life when we "truly" seek meaning from it. It is a gateway to the realm where the Holy Spirit interacts with us and reveals things.

While the Bible is technically published as a "book," it's not a book. Rather, it is a vast collection of God's spiritual teachings for the development of our souls. Through poetry, parable, prayer, some stories of historical narratives and biographies, the Bible teaches about existence, God's nature and ours. It shares extremely valuable, practical and relevant advice. The stories are about real life, people, and relationships. There are farmers and prostitutes, priests and tax collectors, fishermen and lawyers, builders and soldiers. There are extremely loyal people and ruthless, deceitful people, rich people and poor people, hopeless romantics, co-dependents and alcoholics, people with a great deal of integrity and people with very little. One thing they have in common is that they all make mistakes. They all at some point fall into the trap of thinking they can manage life on their own, apart from God's Spirit.

The Bible teaches us how to have healthy marriages, how to address our harmful traits and self-seeking behaviors, how to deal with emotions, conflict, confrontations, disappointment, and betrayal. It teaches us how to live without spiritual malady—that hole inside each of us. And it tells us how to rid our lives of fear. It is far and away the most valuable written source of knowledge we have.

One of the early Apostles wrote, "All Scripture is inspired by God and profitable for teaching, for re-proof, for correction, and training in righteousness, that the man of God may be complete, equipped for every good work." (2 Timothy 3:16-17). There is no disputing that what is in the Bible is profitable for those who are of God.

Another Apostle said that the ultimate origin of Scripture is the Mind of God, "for we did not follow cleverly devised myths when we made known to you the power and coming of our Lord Jesus Christ, but were eyewitness of his majesty... we ourselves heard God's voice on the mountain when He said, 'This is my beloved Son, with whom I am well pleased'..." And we have the prophetic word more fully confirmed... knowing first of all, that no prophecy of Scripture comes from private interpretation. For no prophecy was ever produced by the will of man, but by men of God who spoke as they were moved by the Holy Spirit." (2 Peter 1:16-21, my paraphrase).

I guarantee us all that debating the details of exactly what "divinely inspired" or "breathed out by God" entailed is nothing more than a distraction. Regardless of how the oral teachings of things that were witnessed were retold, captured, and preserved for hundreds of years, then written, debated, and translated, the core messages we will receive, "should we ask," are without a doubt directly from God.

Regardless of how many Isaiahs wrote "Isaiah," or if in fact the gospel of Mark is a recap of Simon Peter's sermon, and if it was Paul or his student who wrote Ephesians, or whether it was Peter or Mary, Mark's mother who wrote "Peter," it is the teaching of Christ that matters.

God said, "So shall My Word be that goes forth from My mouth; It shall not return to Me void (empty or without fruit), But it shall accomplish what I please." (Isaiah 55:11). Scripture works as designed, I have proven it many times for myself. I challenge you to test it for yourself. Read the Bible for 15 minutes every day for one month, sincerely asking God to reveal what you need to know. If you are sincere, I am certain any doubts you have will be replaced with faith. (See Hebrews 11:1.).

Something to pause and think about: There is probably value gained for anyone who reads Shakespeare, but none of us would suggest that a quick read of his works would give us true understanding. In fact, we have college courses and numerous books dedicated to "un-coding" (unraveling) his writing.

The poetry of Isaiah is surely no less wondrous or complex than Shakespeare, but we fail to recognize and appreciate this. The author's use of sentence structure, poetic compression, symbols, metaphor, omission, word play, placement of subject and verb, or inversion of the object before the subject, is no less important in the masterpiece of Isaiah. They are specifically and dare I say supernaturally designed to teach man something, and meaning is that much more compressed with very compact sentences and the use of voice or changing point of view (into the first person).

You cannot give Isaiah a quick read and say, "I've got it," any more than you can read Romeo saying to Juliet, "If I profane with my unworthiest hand this holy shrine," and "What light through yonder window breaks," once without some study of the original language used and the author himself and truly grasp what Shakespeare meant to convey.

Isaiah should be studied, revered, embraced, and appreciated as the master work that it is. Then the same care should be considered when looking at the different poetic styles of say, Solomon or the songs, the prayers and poetry of David in Psalms, or the poetry used in Proverbs and the other works authored in the Bible.

The words from work to work are not used in the same context, so they will likely have different meanings, and as many of Shakespeare's words from the sixteenth century are used differently today, the Bible's words from centuries before Christ are also.

6

READING AND UNDERSTANDING IT FOR YOURSELF: INTERPRETATION

"If you abide in My word, you are truly my disciple"

– JOHN 8:31, ESV

Surely there is a lot of information in the Bible, but interacting with God through it is not purely an intellectual experience: it is an emotional and spiritual one that sometimes expands your mind. It's very bizarre to me that the Bible itself tells us that it is spiritual teaching, and yet so many people ignore that, and read it through the lenses of their concern for the material, visible, and tangible things of the world. The stories, parables, poems, and prayers in the Bible are not designed to teach us the history of Israel, how to "be good," or how to have power over others through organized religion. Rather, they are designed to teach us the truth about ourselves, about existence, and about God, so that we can operate as intended and be effective expressions of God's Spirit, manifesting harmony (love, creative beauty, peace, prosperity, and happiness) – God's will for man.

- The doctrine (teachings) of Jesus explain and/or set straight the meaning of scriptures.
- All interpretation should conform to His teaching. The notion of God that He explained, that's God's nature. The description of who we are, that's the truth about you and me. The interpretations of scripture that He rebuked as corrupt; they are corrupt!
- Each of us should hone our ability to test the validity of meaning and good or evil spirits against the truth of Christ, and not be misled down a false path by another or by our own assumptions.

So, what do we know from studying the Bible? What are some of the things it tells us?

1. Thoughts are the genesis of creation. Thoughts and ideas are spoken into life — be it audible self-talk that defines one's reality, or words verbally spoken. What we say is what we create. We live in our thoughts, which lead to actions.
2. All that God created in and around our world was good. This means that while things (people, powers, principalities, systems, institutions, governments, and offices of authority) might get off track and divert from their purpose, <u>nothing is intrinsically evil</u>.
3. Our true nature is that of a spiritual being. We are the living images of God's Spirit, <u>when we understand that</u>; undivided instances or consciousness of God.
4. Our purpose is to express God's light and love, to reflect the ideas of harmony, creativity, freedom, unity, and love, and to spread these ideas throughout the world, which we have the power (dominion) to do.

5. However, our world is a distorted reality. We have a false notion of God and our existence, a false idea of what we really are. We live under the deception of a lie that we are separated from God, that we are independent beings, and that we must each bear the burden of "managing life" alone, so our focus is on "getting" what we think will make us okay.
6. This creates a self-perpetuating cycle of fear, disharmony, and destruction for the individual and the whole of humanity. We do not operate as designed, but in error (sin), i.e., our software code has defects in it.
7. Since the problem's roots are in our "thoughts," the solution is to change our thoughts, first individually, and then to push that awareness to the whole of humanity (preaching the gospel).
8. Scripture is designed to help us see all of this and implement the necessary change to restore humanity. The Bible provides the actual tools (prayers, meditations, and affirmations) needed to raise one's consciousness and change conditions.
9. Revelations from God to man include the truth of our identity and instructions for operating as designed. The precepts, laws, statutes, promises, and "assuredly I say to you" statements from Jesus are all spiritual truths, natural laws, or consequences that will always follow certain states of mind.

Coming from a technology perspective, I see this as analogous to a software problem: The developer code has defects in it causing the program not to function as designed. Once we see errors (wrong thoughts and beliefs), we can use the correct coding practice (prayer) to modify the code (subconscious belief) so that the software features function as designed (we express God). Once we make the "bug-fix," we can check it into the main code line (our conscious mind) and push the patch or update (right thinking) out to all the devices (people) that run on that code. Then we execute (think and behave) properly.

BASIC INSTRUCTION

If you look at scripture from this perspective, you will see the following pattern:

I. The problem statement (man is not working as designed). These are the concrete tellings of physical happenings.
II. The explanation of the root cause (man's wrong thought). This is the spiritual teaching to do with the lie of self-reliance and fear.
III. The solution (always prayer). The specific instructions on how to overcome fear, realize the presence of the Indwelling Spirit, and call on God's power to positively change conditions.

God talks about a concrete happening or circumstance, like a war between two groups, the literal meaning or the outer aspect, the "what." Then He explains the "why," which is always humankind's wrong thoughts and beliefs. Finally, we are given the solution, the tools to resolve the spiritual, and in turn, the physical difficulty or condition which is always prayer and the realization of the "I AM," our identity in Christ. Actually, as written in its original language, the Bible talks directly about thoughts, which can then produce the physical situation or circumstance. The English language versions focus more on the concrete things, leaving our subconscious mind to process and figure out some of what we call "symbolism."

Interpretation

A good Bible these days will likely include in the preface some basic guidelines about interpretation (understanding what it says and means), but in truth, they are very basic. It's not as simple as reading another book.

In the Bible the word **interpretation** means to unravel or to untie. When we look at the words know, knowledge, and understand, and the various terms they were translated from, we see "wide-open eyes at something remarkable," "to get it," "putting things together," and "to comprehend."

When we read the Bible (which was translated into English) and get the idea that the meaning might not be what it literally seems, e.g. "hand" is not talking about the physical part of our bodies, we are right, not because the Bible was written in metaphorical or symbolic code, but because the translation into the English language took terms speaking about beliefs, thoughts, and states of consciousness, and converted them into English words that are largely concrete. It's the English that creates much of the symbolism. The original Hebrew terms might be full expressions that speak directly and literally about thoughts dispatched from God being delivered to us, which, once conceived in our minds, will change our false beliefs, allowing us to take negative thoughts captive and renew our minds, overcoming fear. When these terms are translated into English, then, we may be left with the images of a concrete story about some man, his enemies, angels, then evildoers, and darkness, leaving our minds to wrestle with what each of these things might symbolize.

The purpose of the scriptures is to teach us about ourselves in relation to God and everything else. They teach us how to love, how to have healthy marriages, how to address our harmful traits and self-seeking behaviors, how to deal with emotions and conflict, confrontations, disappointment, and betrayal. They teach us how to become vessels for Christ.

If we study scripture to understand the spiritual truths God is communicating, we learn that our thoughts and emotions are the main obstacles we face (mine enemies). When we study its "spiritual teachings," we learn to manage ourselves, how to "take our thoughts captive," and "renew our minds." We start to gain dominion over ourselves and the environment around us. Our battles are not physical/concrete things, but with thoughts and beliefs (ours and others). The "sword of the Spirit is the Word of God" (see Ephesians 6:13-17), and it is in the process of studying scripture that His word comes to life in us, and our minds become Christ-like, our beliefs are radically changed through this process, we gain a new perspective, and we are "born again."

The first thing to understand is that meaning is singular. It's common for people to think there can be multiple valid interpretations of a Bible passage (e.g. "this is what it means to me"), but that is false. There is only one correct meaning, and that would be what the author intended to communicate.

There are, however, an unlimited number of ways each of us might apply those teachings in our lives. In other words, God may make known to us a spiritual idea, truth, or law inherent to our nature through scripture, and that would be the meaning; while seeing the various ways it fits our specific situations would be the application.

So how can we tell for sure what the author meant? The basic instruction I was given when I first started studying scripture was to "read in context," meaning reading verses before and after what you're focused on, and expanding out to other chapters within the book in the hope that you will see clearly what is being communicated.

What I discovered is that reading the English translation of the Bible absent an understanding of the meaning of the original ancient Hebrew or Greek creates a lot of room for misinterpretation or misunderstanding.

For example, I might assume that I know what an English word means, but there were 15 different Hebrew and Greek terms that translators reduced to that one English word, so lost in translation is the specific context. Alternatively, there could be one Hebrew term, like *dabar*, which might then be translated into two different English words such as "things" and "words" in the very same passage of Scripture.

- The scriptures of the Old Testament and New Testament in the original writings (manuscripts) are the inspired word of God and are error free.
- This by no means suggests that men, even religious men, have not at times misappropriated, misinterpreted, or perverted their meanings, for they most certainly have. There are over 200 different English translations (Protestant, Catholic, Mormon, and Jehovah's Witness-sponsored).
- Christ is the authority on the interpretation of all Bible scripture. If your understanding of a verse is not in line with His teaching, then you don't have the correct understanding. My suggestion here is that you look up the entire verse word for word in a concordance to verify that you understand what is being communicated.
- A concordance is a book that identifies the original Hebrew, Aramaic, or Greek terms used in place of an English word you're reading. You can see the definition of the term that was originally used.

Word Definitions & Bible Symbolism

Let's take a look at our understanding of words and symbols as it relates to better comprehension of the Bible. Many times, we misunderstand the correct meaning of standard words in our English language. On top of that, without looking up the original Hebrew term used in a specific passage, we are not likely to have an accurate understanding of its intended meaning.

- For example, the word **individual** does not equate to a separate entity. "Separate" means to break apart or to disconnect. An individual is the opposite of that. It literally means undivided – it is an instance of something connected; a part of; undivided from. Our use of that word has changed over time to meaning a separate person.

Integrity means to be whole. It comes from the root word "integration." To be whole, we must be fully integrated. Our beliefs, thoughts, and actions must line up with core our values, and we must be integrated with those with whom we share the world.

- **Ego** is frequently thought of as a psychoanalytic term having to do with pride or self-esteem, when in fact it is the sense of self as distinguished from other things, the idea of "me."
- A **Genius** is not a super-smart person, but rather knowledge from God, shared via a message/messenger (angel). The Merriam-Webster Dictionary from 2016 defines Genius as "an attendant Spirit," "a supernatural intellect," or a "tutelary spirit" (guardian angel).
- Being **Vain** is most frequently thought of as being proud of one's looks. The primary meaning of the word has to do with feeling empty, futile, or worthless.
- **Religion** originally meant the "service and worship of God." It is commonly hijacked as used as "devotion to an institutionalized system of beliefs, attitudes, and practices (man's stuff).

- **Theology** as a word means "the study of God in relation to the world." Institutionalized Christianity, the ancient Catholic Church, encouraged that to morph into the study of "their doctrine, theory, and tradition of religious practices," as they declared "tradition superior to scripture" and then defined theories of what scripture meant. Many of those theories and doctrines are just accepted because that's what has been taught historically (and still is to a large degree).

A sample of English words vs. terms originally used in scripture

- **Kill, destroy, punish, death, vengeance,** and **jealous**, for example, are all English words we associate with violence and harshness in connection with God in the Old Testament. The terms originally used have a very different tone and meaning than we assume.
- Of the five or so terms in the Old Testament that were translated into the English words punish or punished, only one has to do with our typical notion of the word (to strike, harm, or exact revenge), and God is not connected to its use. The dialogue about "God punishing" has nothing to do with harming. The terms describe God visiting, instructing, urging, retraining, and spoiling our destructive ideas.

  Punish in the Old Testament Hebrew:

  - *yacar* – instruct
  - *anash* – urge
  - *raa* – to spoil
  - *nakah* – to strike

- The word **destroy** has to do with terms about "rendering something ineffective" to have influence over us.

- **Enemies** are thoughts in opposition to you, or hateful ideas (your thoughts or other people's).
- The ancient Hebrew terms translated into **vengeance** have to do with vindication. "God will come with vengeance," actually means something like, God will help you overcome other people's judgement and assassination of your character, and you will be vindicated in that you will no longer have your self-esteem or identity attached to receiving acceptance and validation from other people.
- The terms involving **fear of God** mean respecting, having reverence for, or appreciating who and what God is, not anything to do with fear as in fight or flight alarms or terror. The Bible is actually very clear that "fear" is the output of Satan's lie that we can't trust God.
- In the Bible, to **believe**, means "to know something is." To have **faith** is not to have "blind hope," but "to have persuasive evidence of something not seen."
- Of the five terms translated into the English word **heart**, only one has to do with the blood-pumping organ. The rest mostly have to do with the subconscious mind (feelings, memories, beliefs, intellect) and thoughts. Out of the one hundred and five times *heart* appears in the New Testament, the *organ* term only occurs twice. There are about fourteen terms which were reduced to the word **mind**, some of which are the same term used for heart, while the others have to do with the "soundness or state of one's mind," beliefs, and opinions.

Bible Symbolism & Idiom

Ancient Hebrew didn't separate spirit from matter, and much of the Greek New Testament wrote about both the inner and outer aspects of something at the same time. In the English-speaking Bible, things we can't experience through our five senses are most frequently discussed metaphorically. Things that cannot be seen or touched, such as thoughts, beliefs, faith, or mental states are discussed figuratively. Using the *Strong's Exhaustive Concordance* with dictionaries of Hebrew and Greek terms will provide the literal meaning so you can verify that you have the correct understanding of a metaphor. In just a minute we'll see this illustrated by walking through some passages of the Bible. Then you can try it for yourself in example exercises.

Here's a sample list of some symbols and their meaning:

- **Child** frequently stands for an idea that is new to you. Once conceived in your soul, you have grasped and internalized it.
- **Son**, "the builder of the family name," is our identity, our notion of who and what we are.
- The **name** of anything is not just an arbitrary way to identify it (a label) but means the character or nature of that thing. A person's name is a hieroglyph of their soul.
- **Water** is the human soul. **Seas** are turbulent emotions and human personality. **River** stands for purpose (not drifting or floating but moving along the path).
- The **Secret place of the Most High**, the **Upper Room**, etc. is your highest level of conscious thought, the ascending state of mind.
- **Mountain** generally means prayer; the uplifted consciousness.
- In the Old Testament, the **City of God** is mankind's consciousness. Your reality is your city. In the New Testament, it most frequently refers to spiritual warfare.
- **Hands** are strength and the power of thought, usually referring to expressing God's ideas; the power to manifest God's Spirit on the physical plane.

- **Earth** means manifestation or expression.
- **Israel** stands for the idea that God will rule.
- **Jerusalem** means the teaching founded in peace.
- **New Jerusalem** stands for the awakened consciousness, the awareness of God's Truth, and the freedom from the deception of Satan's lie.
- **Heart**, as already mentioned, usually stands for the subconscious mind (one that needs to be redeemed and re-educated from the errors that have accumulated over time).
- **Egypt** means limitation (upper and lower); consciously and unconsciously accepting ideas of human limitation (we can't, it won't work, I can't overcome an obstacle or situation, etc.).
- **Shadow**, in most cases, is the false belief in death (shadow of death), not the death of the real self, but physical death and the ego's notion that we are not eternal.
- **Dragon** or **Jackal** can refer to a set of complex ideas heavily charged with emotion and hidden in the subconscious mind ("complexes").
- Symbolically, **wicked** and **mine enemies** are thoughts, fears and doubts. In general, the Hebrew terms translated into the English word wicked are referring to the spell of deception under which society operates (Satan's lie).
- **Gates** and **Doors** are paths to understanding.
- **Promise** is a statement of spiritual truth inherent to us as beings. God's promise is a statement of consequences (positive or negative) that will naturally follow certain states of mind, such as meditating on the presence of God within you.

7

INSTITUTIONALIZED RELIGION AND DOCTRINE VS. THE TEACHINGS OF JESUS

In good conscience I must speak plainly about church history, Catholicism, and Orthodox Christianity, and of what is "Christian doctrine" vs. what Christianity was and is meant to be.

God asks, "why do you not understand My speech"

JOHN 8:43

There was what Jesus taught while on earth, and what He trained His disciples to teach. That doctrine was captured in the New Testament by some of the early disciples and apostles, the men and women who planted the first Christian churches, spread Christianity through Africa, the Middle East, the Mediterranean, and Italy, and were murdered by the Roman military because of it.

For decades after the ascension of Jesus, Christ's teachings were still being spread, "His doctrine," His movement occurring. During that time, Christian services were mostly held in homes. The Roman emperor Nero (54-68 CE) for example, aggressively persecuted Christians, holding public burnings as forms of entertainment for citizens and as a means of execution.

The Apostle Paul went on several church planting missions between A.D. 46-57, traveling throughout Turkey and Greece, which became the hub for church planting and evangelism throughout the Roman province of Asia (current day Turkey). This region was an empire of cities filled with various groups of people, cultures, and languages, lending itself well to the model of independent, local, self-governing churches equipped to minister to their communities. Each city had a bishop of its own, assisted by priests and deacons.

As churches started to spread throughout that region, the Christ-follower movement faced lots of internal struggles as differing and false doctrine (counter to what Christ taught) was developed and used in churches by bishops and priests, who in their thirst for status and power sought to establish themselves and developed their theories. Most of those men were killed because of their faith. This pattern of heated debate by passionate men willing to risk their lives for what they believed in, coupled with subversive desire for personal status, continued to occur from the 100s on.

We can look at two historical documents to get a feel for the dynamic in the 100 years that followed Jesus; the Letter of Ignatius to the Smyrnians (A.D. 107-110), and the Letter from Governor Pliny to Emperor Trajan (A.D. 112).

Ignatius of Antioch was the bishop (overseer of churches) in that area. While being transported to a Roman gladiator's arena where he would be killed by lions for entertainment, he stopped in the city of Smyrna. There, he wrote a letter of direction on the authority of the church and gave it to the local Christian leaders who visited him. He used the word "catholic" in describing the idea of a single organization which would serve as the "universal church" (the meaning of the word catholic). In this letter he made a case for a hierarchy in which bishops would function as "Christ on earth." Here are some excerpts from his letter: "See that you follow the bishop – even as Jesus Christ followed the Father;" "let no man do anything connected with the church without the bishop;" "It is not lawful either to baptize or celebrate without the bishop;""whatever the bishop approved is pleasing to God."(*The Epistle of Ignatius to the Smyrnaens, Ante-Nicene Library (Edinburgh: T&T Clark, 1867).*

In Governor Pliny's letter to Emperor Trajan, he asked how to deal with Christians from a criminal standpoint. He told his boss that he'd been executing those who admitted to being Christian but giving them a chance to deny or renounce that faith and sparing them if they did. The emperor told him he was handling it correctly, and counseled him not to waste time creating suspect lists and seeking them out, but rather to address just the ones who were directly accused by a Roman citizen. – see *The Letter of Governor Pliny to Emperor Trajan in The Genuine Works of Flavius Josephus, translation by William Whiston (Worstcester, MA: Isaiah Thomas, 1974).*

The Apostle John, who was a leader of the early Christ-follower movement and the author of the books of John and Revelation, was ministering to the churches of Asia for many years after Paul went to prison. While John was serving 18 months in prison on the Island of Patmos, God provided him with an understanding (revelation) about the spiritual conflict these churches were engaged in, and gave him some insight into the continuum of spiritual warfare which humanity contends with, showing us that Satan (the spirit in opposition to the truth of our identity) comes together around the notions of power that society creates (institutionalized religion, ideologies, and societal powers). Christ also gave John direction and encouragement to share with the churches of Asia, telling of His return, the end of "the lie's" effectiveness, and the total reconciliation that would come. There would be no more thoughts of being unwanted, unworthy, not enough, or unloved. There would be no fear, total forgiveness, and an embracing of His love. Humanity would get it – all would see the Truth that they were loved Beings, made to be expressions of God. The spiritual truth taught in the book of Revelation is extremely profound, and warrants a close look, which we will take later.

The followers, apostles, disciples, and saints were still being brutally killed by Roman soldiers up until about A.D. 315. The emperor Constantine had an encounter in A.D. 312 and converted to Christianity. In 313 he issued an Edict of religious toleration that gave Christians full legal rights and freedom to worship. Constantine moved the capital of the Roman Empire to Istanbul, Turkey and named the city after himself (Constantinople). In A.D. 325 Constantine held the council of Necia in an effort to forge unity among all the bishops and establish some agreement on a centralized theology and doctrine. The output was a common creed. In an effort to unify the pagan and Christian people of his empire, he also adopted the Pagan day of worship (Sunday) as the empire's official day of rest and worship for all religions, changing Christian church services from Saturday (sabbath) to Sunday.

Constantinus II (337-361) banned the Creed of Necia and adopted a new statement that the Son (Jesus) was no longer that same substance as the Father (e.g. Jesus was less than God). At a council in 341, a total distinction between the Father and Son was declared.

The pagan Roman emperor, Julian the Apostate (361-363) disavowed the Catholic Church, and Christians alone were eligible for citizenship. Once the capital of the Empire was moved back to Rome under Justinian, the Roman Catholic Church made its push for the Bishop of Rome (which had been Peter's role) to hold the sole earthly position of supremacy (Pope).

From that point on the Christian church movement was assimilated into the newly Holy Roman Empire (the merging of the Empire and Christianity) – the very power that for hundreds of years had been oppressing, persecuting, and killing people (the very things Christ taught against). Jesus's Christianity faded, and "Christianity" became what the Catholic Church said it was, as wealthy and aristocratic people became the congregations of focus, and new intellectual church leaders strived to swallow up the existing churches movement into the **institutional power** (the term *basileus* in Greek) they were building within the Roman Empire's constructs. The Church then did exactly what Jesus taught against by creating a hierarchical religious power governed by its own tradition, distorting His instruction, and coming up with interpretations of scripture to support the perception they were creating – that their Church was the holy "infallible" and all powerful entity to whom God had given authority to regulate faith for all men. Religious leaders were able to get emperors to create laws to persecute those who opposed their views (heretics) – and the emperors were able to get religious leaders to teach in a way that supported the Empire's causes, thereby "teaching as doctrine the commandments of men" and "making the word of God void in favor of their traditions." (Matthew 15:1-9).

WE ARE WARNED ABOUT RELIGION'S FALSE TEACHING

For three hundred years following the resurrection of Christ, believers refused to engage in war. Once Christianity was embraced (taken over) by the Roman Empire, there was a rationalization within the "church" that participating in violence and oppression of "their nation's" enemies was just. **That is not a teaching from Christ**, but rather from the Babylonian creation story, the Enamu Elish; the myth that violence can be redemptive. The idea that good can restore order by destroying evil—that the hero kills the bad guy and saves the day—is in fact "anti" Christ's teaching. Jesus taught us to "love" our enemies. He told us to confront injustice, ignorance, and evil, but non-violently. He explained that responding to evil with evil, to violence with violence, or to hate with hate would simply cause both sides to perpetuate evil.

When the Roman Empire embraced Christianity, one of the results was victory of the empire over the power and freedom for people found in the gospel Jesus taught. The church ceased being the persecuted and became a persecutor, thus following the anti-Christ without being consciously aware of it. The Bible prophesies about this in the book of Revelation.

Tertullian was one of the first Catholic priests who was a leader at the Church of Carthage before the Roman Empire took over. He was a criminal attorney who became a Christ follower in his 40s, writing many times to the Roman Empire imploring them to stop persecuting, imprisoning, and killing Christians without so much as a trail to convict them of any crime. A hundred and fifty years after the ascension of Jesus, Tertullian was telling Roman soldiers who converted to Christianity to "quit their jobs or be prepared to die as martyrs because followers of Christ do not kill." He then wrote against "the church" with more fervor than he had against the Roman persecutors, as he watched what he thought was hypocrisy and anti-Christ behavior among Christian leaders, and against one bishop, who later became Pope Callistus.

Then we have the famous Aurelius Augustine for example, more than two hundred years later, writing to the opposite of Tertullian, with a theory of "just war," where God condones violence as long as there's a "good reason," such as the Roman Empire's cause, or a Church leader's agenda for that matter. Augustine persuaded the

Emperor Hororius to create cruel and persecuting laws against all who disagreed with his opinions, including fellow bishops with differing interpretations of scripture.

Heresy [*hairesis* in Greek] as a word in the Bible means **choice**. It is used in the context of making a choice to follow God or to follow man's traditions. The Catholic Church and later the Church of England twisted our understanding of that word's meaning to "choosing anything other than their church's statements, positions, or interpretations." A common English dictionary today would define the word as "believing a religious opinion or doctrine contrary to church doctrine." **Heresy** is not "questioning the views or teachings of a church," **it is following teachings that go against what Jesus taught, said, and demonstrated.** My allegiance is to Christ, not to a religious organization.

I've been able to read a lot of the detailed histories of doctrinal controversies within the ancient Catholic Church, and then of Protestant theology – the confession of faith documents I mentioned earlier – as well as the writing of men like Tertullian and Augustine to see for myself what they actually taught. I am left with a clear reminder that Christ's teaching is Divine, but our interpretation can be very much human. Between Augustine's book *Confessions*, written by himself, and the biography written by his disciple and friend of forty years, Possidius, Bishop of Calama in Numidia, we can see as much fallen man as we can gifted, talented servant.

I'm not picking on Augustine with malicious intent, as we know that God uses broken people to demonstrate His glory, but there are also ongoing spiritual battles where people try to use God to glorify themselves. Augustine, who was born in North Africa, for example, first studied and believed in Greek mythology, and then spent nine years as a Manichaen, a religion born in modern-day Baghdad, before converting to Christianity. In his book *Confessions*, he candidly talked about the errors of his youth, his struggles with alcohol, sobriety, sex, and his violent temper. He talked about praying to God for chastity, "but not too soon." He had a son out of wedlock at age eighteen and took a second concubine after becoming a Christian. In short, he sounds very much like many alcoholics I have known, which is not a negative statement—he did find sobriety. I am merely saying he was not above anyone else in morals or behavior over the course of his life.

Languages were Augustine's weak point as a scholar. He had an aversion to Greek and never attempted to learn Hebrew, and yet his opinions on interpretation of Scripture (written in those languages) were accepted by the Catholic Church. He was an eloquent and persuasive speaker and a rhetoric teacher. Late in his life, he acknowledged that his reliance on the Latin translation of the Bible (Vulgate) was a problem, as he frequently found himself in arguments about erroneous interpretations. The Vulgate was the only translation that the Roman Catholic Church recognized between the third and twentieth centuries. The Latin translation was first done in the second century A.D. and completed by Jerome in A.D. 405, under the direction of Damasus, bishop of Rome. Augustine's mentor St. Ambrose told him that Latin was not to be read literally, but rather symbolically.

By the fifth century, which marked the fall of the Roman Empire, the Church began going through major changes on positions about everything supernatural. A thousand years before the first printing of the Bibles (Old Testament and New Testament), reincarnation, which had been accepted for hundreds of years by Christians, was condemned by the Catholic Church in 553 A.D. at the Second Council of Constantinople, and the supernatural and working of miracles by the common person started to become sins of idolatry. The Holy Roman Empire was in place (see Daniel 7:24-25 and Revelation 17:12-13). A lot of things occurred between the sixth and fourteenth century (which I cover in another book), but for our purposes let's skip ahead.

In 1326, Pope John Paul XXII proclaimed sorcery a crime and the Catholic Church applied the term "witchcraft" to all supernatural or psychic abilities and to anything that might today be called paranormal (that which cannot be explained through normal understanding). Then around 1484, two Dominican priests wrote the *Malleus Maleficarum* (the Hammer of Witches), and with the Pope's approval, the authors became inquisitors. For the next 200 years, their book was the manual for witch hunters. Over the next several centuries, hundreds of thousands of people were tortured and executed as witches. Approximately eighty-five percent were widowed, unmarried, or older women. The Church declared a battle against the devil, and witches had to be destroyed. Use of any "spiritual gift" (healing, performing miracles, discerning spirits, speaking in tongues, or prophesying) was risky business, to say the least. It's the same story as when Jesus tells the scribes and Pharisees that they were "perverting scripture and His will".

In the 1520s, England began its religious Reformation. Under King Henry VIII, a revolution began turning England from a medieval Catholic society into a Protestant state, eventually breaking ties with Rome and the people, and making the King of England the head of the Church of England. The power struggle between Protestants and Catholics went back and forth. After King Henry there was Queen Mary, an ardent Catholic who earned the name "Bloody Mary" for burning Protestants at the stake as heretics. Then came Queen Elizabeth I, who returned to the Reformation efforts of Henry, making Catholicism a no-no once again. Under her "Protestant" rule, the Puritans did an equally ruthless amount of hunting down and executing of Catholics.

Before Constantine, the Christians were persecuted by the Romans. Then the Romans took over Christianity, the Church persecuted believers as witches, then later on persecuted denominations of itself, with Catholics and Protestant Christians killing each other in the name of God.

The notion of miracles was such an issue for the Catholic Church that back in Rome in the 1730s, Cardinal Prospero Lambertini (before he became Pope Benedict XIV) wrote a report of the Criterium of Supernatural that classified which events would be considered miracles attributed to God, and which phenomena would be deemed products of the mind. He said that telepathy, clairvoyance, many healings, and some prophecies were not miracles, while stigmata, bilocation, certain healings, incorruptibility, Marian apparitions, and "divine images" of Jesus were miracles. In essence, what Lambertini classified as miracles were events of God's own volition, rather than humans petitioning God and God working through us, as Jesus instructed us to do. It made "miracles" things that God did independently from us, removing human participation, and making us passive as it related to prayer and calling on God's power. This is subtle, but hugely significant. Jesus told us to put our hands on sick people, praying in His name (believing in Him and all that He said) and the people would be healed. He told us to perform miracles as He did. Men, then, leaders with the holy Roman Church, told us not to take Christ's teachings too literally, and relegated the degree of believers' influence to works of service.

Works of service, generosity, loving acts of kindness, and personal sacrifice are certainly key parts of Christ's teaching, and they are the tangible, rational, healing acts we can perform, but they are not the supernatural ones that Jesus also commanded us to do.

Do "we" (the church) not believe Jesus when He says we can achieve the same miracles He did? If so, isn't that the unbelief that Paul warns about when he says, "But I fear, lest somehow, as the serpent deceived Eve by craftiness, so your minds may be corrupted from the simplicity that is Christ. For if he who comes preaches another Jesus ...or a different gospel which you have not accepted -- you may well put up with it." (2 Corinthians 11:3-4).

In reading the "Catechism of the Catholic Church," the book that details its guiding traditions or rules, and the Professional of Faith that the Catholic Church says one must believe in order to receive salvation, one can readily see where men, Catholic bishops such as St. Augustine, St. Thomas Aquinas, St. Irenaeus, St. John Chrystom, St. Gregory (Pope), St. Leo "the great" (Pope), and Pope Pisus inserted their "own ideas" beyond what was contained in scripture into the meaning of it, declaring themselves as intermediaries between man and God.

From the fourth century on, at the councils of Ephesus, Orange, Mentz, Necia, Trent, the Lateran council, the Vatican council and the Council of Constantinople – many interpretations, theories, and traditions were agreed to as "doctrine" of the Church. Some of this tradition and doctrine is a pretty extreme departure from my understanding of what "Christ" was teaching, and while there are many Christian denominations that do not endorse Catholicism, some of the "doctrine" developed in the ancient Catholic Church is still accepted as Christian today, when in actuality it is "anti" Christ's teaching.

Rituals created by the Catholic Church

- A.D. 320 Sunday laws enforced, changing worship services from the Sabbath (Saturday) to Sunday
- A.D. 450 Death sentence for Sabbath-keepers
- A.D. 593 Creation of the concept of Purgatory
- A.D. 600 The Latin language alone was to be used for prayer and worship; prayers were directed to Mary and dead men (saints)

- A.D. 607 The title of Pope was used
- A.D. 709 Kissing of the Pope's feet
- A.D. 927 College of Cardinals
- A.D. 995 Canonizing of dead men as Saints
- A.D 1090 Rosary and mechanical prayer with beads (the opposite of what Jesus taught about prayer)
- A.D. 1190 Sales of Indulgences (buying absolution of sin and God's forgiveness from the Church)
- A.D. 1215 Auricular Confession of sins to a priest instead of to God
- A.D. 1229 Bible officially forbidden for laymen to read (on the index of "forbidden books")
- A.D. 1545 Tradition (sayings of Catholic leaders) officially declared greater than scripture

The most egregious ones being:

- That Christ empowered Peter alone as the one person with exclusive authority to "bind and loosen;" that he alone was given "the keys to the kingdom of heaven;" that the office of the People then as the successor to the last role Peter held (bishop of Rome) gave the Pope the power to declare interpretations, doctrine, and traditions as holy
- That the Catholic Church was an "infallible" entity apart from the body of believers.
- That Catholic bishops were the elected successors to Christ's chosen Apostles, and only through their church could forgiveness, baptism, and salvation be granted.
- One must put "faith in the Church."
- Mary was the model of faith and love for humanity to follow (not Jesus)

- The concept of "just war"
- Man's tradition was supreme to Scripture

When we read the teachings of Jesus in the Bible we can plainly see:

- Killing is not a godly approach to your enemies. God teaches us to "love them."
- Christ gave all believers "the keys to the kingdom of heaven," and the ability to bind and loosen is available to those who come together in agreement in prayer (with total belief, expectation, and thankfulness).
- Christ teaches that no man should be called father or teacher, that the church is the collective of all believers, NOT an organization.
- He teaches that there are NO intermediaries between God and an individual, that God literally exists in each of us (if we receive Him).
- He instructs all believers to baptize, heal, and preach (share the message of the gospel), and says that if you don't do these things, you don't love Him.
- Lastly, He is the proto-type for humanity. We are instructed to think, act, pray, and love like He does.

It is important for us to acknowledge that the "Church" is the body of Christ (all of us believers), not an organization. And that the Church as an institution has been as fallen and idolatrous as any other organization in society.

I've said this earlier, but it's worth hammering on because it seems that many people are tentative or confused about Jesus as the Son of God, and also God Himself. "God is the Father, the Son, and the Holy Spirit." This means there's no room for discrepancy between how Jesus says things are and how God means them to be. They are one and the same. Jesus is the exact imprint of God's nature, the "exact" character or representation of God's person (Hebrews 1:3). Of the Son, God says, "Your throne, O God, is forever and forever..."(Hebrews 1:8). Jesus said, "I am the way, and the truth, and the life. No man comes to the Father except through Me. If you had known Me, you would have known the Father also. From now on you do know Him and you have seen Him." (John 14:6-7). "... God spoke to our fathers by prophets, but in these last days He has spoken to us by His Son." (Hebrews 1:1). Jesus said, "I and the Father are one." (John 10:30).

If I handed you an addendum to a legal agreement and it stated that it "superseded" the original document, I don't think you would have any trouble understanding that what the addendum said in either correcting or modifying any terms or conditions of the original contract made the original null and void. This is a good analogy for Jesus's doctrine. His teaching was the addendum to mankind's understanding of scripture, correcting our false notion of God and of our existence as beings – exposing the deception under which the world lived. Jesus specifically taught that "capital punishment" and "just war" were not valid understandings of God's instructions, but perversions of their meaning and part of Satan's manipulative, subversive methods of perpetuating "the lie."

Some theologians would debate that Exodus 12:15-24 indicate that capital punishment (an eye for an eye) and mortal combat in war were condoned by God if there was a "good cause." I would say that when you interpret Exodus that way, it says that God suggests killing women who commit adultery, people who dishonor their parents, and those who intentionally kill others (in other words, 80% of all married women, most people who have parents, and many soldiers). I would say this is "anti-Christ" teaching.

It does not matter what we think Exodus or Ezekiel meant to say, because Jesus said, "that's not how it is," and that's what Christianity is meant to be, believing in what Christ said, taught and did, believing in His name—not "yeah, but the Old Testament says something different"—that is the lie. God is not a cruel, violent killer; He is trustworthy. Anytime we don't take God (Christ) at His word, but attempt to modify or suppress His teaching, we are doing it out of fear, following "the lie." The lie, fear, is extremely subversive.

We should absolutely respect the efforts of those who dedicate themselves to serving God, and who come alongside us, aiding our spiritual development, and sometimes investing in us personally, and at the same time we can be careful not to forget that Christ alone is our Father and Teacher. With appreciation for the man Pope Francis is, a good man, a loving man I assume, he is still a man and not our Holy Father. In fact, those who call him, or any priest "father" are engaging in anti-Christ behavior in setting him above themselves, and between Christ and man. Jesus said, "call no one of earth Father, but the Father whom we have in the heavens." (Matthew 23:9).

As "Christians," believers in Christ, we are called to be examples of good. Nonetheless, we all fall short. None of us should simply accept a position without carefully looking at the ramifications. In writing about the attitudes that those who study scripture should have, Ellen White reminds us, "we must study the truth for ourselves. No living man should be relied upon to think for us. No matter who it is, or what position he may be placed in, we are not to look upon any man as perfect criterion for us."

> *"I will delight myself in thy statutes: I will not forget thy word." – Psalm 119:16 KJV*

THEOLOGY

An observation: **theology**, the study of God, works when it is a personal exploration of God's nature in relation to us and the world at large; when through direct experiences, you encounter truth and see where that truth applies to your personal situation, experience, and the world around you. It does not work when theology is the study of God by learning another person's (a theologian's) interpretations of what scripture said, and theories of religious practices that they create in response to their understanding. What if the other person misunderstands? Even if they do understand, how can they make you believe with conviction something they've experienced or seen? Belief, true belief, is one of those "you'd have to be there" situations. One must encounter God or truth oneself in order for it to become "truth" for them. These things are not tangible.

If I had the correct understanding of scripture, and we could do a weekend-long workshop together where I could explain all of the concepts that the Bible teaches, and you understood them all, that would be a misuse of our weekend, a misdirected effort. Now, if I was able to share some ideas, a little of what I've experienced and seen in studying scripture, and exposed you to some tools or methods to explore it for yourself, and you spent the majority of the weekend studying, exploring and praying, and at the end shared what you found out with the group, that would be a blessed weekend.

My intention is that we honor the Father in following Christ's teaching, in learning Scripture for ourselves, and not in accepting misinformation, and in realizing that we can be called to spiritual action. We are called to "believe," not to wait passively for God to do it alone. He gave us dominion. We are humble, but not weak nor powerless. We are made in God's likeness!

The book of Revelation, Babylon the great, and the Scarlet Beast

> *"Now the Spirit speaketh expressly, that in the later times some shall depart from faith, giving heed to seducing spirits and doctrine of devils; speaking lies in hypocrisy..."—1 Timothy 4:1-2 KJV*

I had always known the book of Revelation to be where the apocalypse, "the end of the world" as we know it, is talked about, and where God judges the good, who go to heaven, and the evil, who go to hell. It turns out that was a little naïve on my part. The Greek term used was *Apokalypsis*, which means "disclosure" or "unveiling." Revelation is just that: God showing us the Truth and exposing Satan's lie, once and for all.

In the past, I attempted to make sense of all the symbolism in Revelation by reading Bible commentaries on it, and then rereading the English words with my new assumptions of the meaning behind them and not really getting that the English translators created the confusing symbolic dialogue through their process and choices. I also read my study Bible, which clued me in that Babylon in the New Testament was a veiled reference to Rome. In studying this way, I was able to see a more complicated version of the same story I'd heard in bits and pieces throughout my life, but honestly, it was still confusing.

When I looked up every Greek term originally used and its meaning (as is my practice today) the teaching about spiritual truths inherent to our nature as beings was not difficult to see or understand. Nonetheless, I was shocked on more than one occasion. What I saw probably didn't surprise me as much as it might have surprised others because it was further confirmation of what I had been seeing and writing about over the last two years.

I want to acknowledge upfront that what I share here may be disturbing for some people. Some may feel that they have been "lied to," while others may feel compelled to respond with defensiveness, dismissing what I see as "wrong." Some people, I hope, will be relieved to see clarity around what they kind of suspected but could not put their finger on. With this is mind, I am simply presenting the information I see in using the Strong's Exhaustive Concordance with the King James and New King James versions of the Bible to look up the Greek terms "actually used" and their meaning. This way you can look it up for yourself and determine if you see what I do. If you want more detail, you can also look at the Thayer's Greek-English Lexicon of the New Testament, which I have also utilized here.

We're just going to focus closely on a few sections together, but I have a book coming out dedicated to looking at all of Revelation and encourage you to study the whole of Revelation on your own at some point.

When I look up the original terms used, I see Revelation making total sense.

Some of what I see:

- God told John to write the things He showed him in a book and send it to the seven churches which were in Asia (current day Turkey).
- God points out the spiritual things going wrong in those churches – false teaching; vilifying of Gods nature; priests and congregants who claim to be followers of Christ, and are not, but are the church of Satan; the embracing of the spirit of abandonment and unworthiness, who teaches us we'll be okay if we perform well, if we gain personal power, influence, and acceptance.
- God explains the shadiness that hides the Truth of God; "retails and adulterates people" (the meaning for the Greek

terms translated into smoke from the bottomless pit and darkened – see Revelation 90.

- God tells John to "seal up" those lies and false ideas that were being propagated (the seven thunders uttered – see Revelation 10:4).
- I also see God telling of two kinds of churches – the small persecuted one, the true movement of Christ – and the big false church, the one of institutionalized religion.

> *"For God is not the author of confusion, but of peace, as in all the churches of Saints" – 1 Corinthians 4:33*

According to scripture, there are actually NO contradictions in the Bible; there's inconsistency or confusion in what God is continuously teaching us. Our confusion (the meaning of the word Babylon) and misunderstanding occur when we as a society are manipulated into seeing what Satan wants us to see.

> *"And the great dragon was cast out, that old serpent, called the Devil, and Satan **which deceiveth the whole world...**" –Revelation 12:9*

God tells us to prove all things, while Satan deceives us by getting us to accept things without proving (see 1 Thessalonians 5:21). Think for a moment about all that you blindly accept as truth, what's on the Internet, what you see on TV, the sound bites of information intentionally shoved at you so that you will conform to the spirit in opposition to God.

Believe it or not, the book of Revelation teaches us that it's actually through institutionalized religion that Satan accomplished most of his deception. Let's take a look for ourselves.

In Revelation 17, one of the angels shows John how Satan (the scarlet beast) is the spirit behind the perpetuation of "the lie," a.k.a Babylon. The word Babylon means **to confuse or to confound**. Revelation teaches us that the *incarnation of Babylon occurs when man attempts to create foundations of power to regulate people's beliefs, opinions, and or understanding of faith; to control people's perception of Truth and our ability to see God in our life moment by moment.* This is accomplished by blasphemy or vilifying God's nature. Through lies, rumors or false teachings, Satan get us to see God as untrustworthy. This then reinforces harlotry or the promotion of idolatry, which means placing our trust in personal power and things that society says will give us security and fulfillment, such as acceptance, status, popularity, money, or physical might—the ability to influence and control things. The "lie" tells us that if we can perform well in acquiring these things, we will then be okay (worthy of love, safe, and wanted). Regulating faith or belief allows the spirit behind an institution to neutralize God's instructions. It allows for false teaching and the rendering of believers ineffective to effect change across humanity (Dominion, to spread God's reign). It's Satan's master plan to keep us from spreading salvation—to keep people confused.

The term **hell** (*hades* in Greek) literally translates as "unseen." It comes from the two terms "alpha" and "to see or perceive." So hell as the Bible describes it is the state of not perceiving God as a reality working in your life on earth, and not seeing Him in the afterlife. It's a state of mind, which then affects your whole outlook (fountain), your body, the choices you make and which circumstances or conditions you yield to as having power and authority over your life.

What you believe in and see as true at the end of this earth-human-form experience is what your spiritual self takes into the next dimension. There have been all kinds of literature over hundreds of years (such as Dante's *Inferno*) proposing notions of hell as a destination where one is eternally tortured, a lake of fire, etc. But if we, each of us, look at the actual meaning of Bible scripture for ourselves, we will get a difference picture (study Revelation 21).

Revelation 17:1-2 talks about "the great whore who sits on many waters, with whom the kings of the earth committed fornication and the inhabitants of the earth were made drunk with the wine of her fornication."

When we look at the Greek words used and their meaning, we see that the word **Kings** was used in place of a Greek term *basileus* (Strong's #935), meaning "notions of a foundation of power," i.e. institutions, not the ruler of a kingdom. **Fornication** is the Greek word *poreuo* (Strong's #4203), meaning "to act the harlot, to permit oneself to be drawn away by another," to be given to idolatry or "placing trust in things that you think will give you power." **Great** is the Greek word *megas* [Strong's 3173], generically meaning big. Here it is used in the context of "the external appearance of things; being perceived as big; highly esteemed and important," while full of arrogance and presumptuous things that are derogatory to the majesty of God. It's interesting that Americans generally seem to think big is good (megachurch).

- See pages 394-395 of Thayer's Greek-English Lexicon of the New Testament, copyright @ 1977, Baker Book House Company.

Water is the word *hudor* (Strong's #5204), symbolically meaning souls. **Drink** and **Wine,** *methuo* and *onios* (Strong's #3184 and #3631) are speaking about drinking what's being served (lies, societies' ideals, church doctrine) to the point of being intoxicated and enticed by them.

So far, "Kings" means the foundations of power of institutions man creates—and "Hell" is the state of not perceiving God. These things I saw got me feeling as if the translation of Revelation into English was a bit misleading, but it was in Revelation 17:3-5 where my mouth literally dropped open in shock.

Revelation 17:3-5 says, "And I saw a woman sitting on a scarlet beast which was full of **names** of **blasphemy**...," "and on her **forehead** a name was written: **MYSTERY, BABYLON THE GREAT,** THE **MOTHER** OF **HARLOTS** AND THE **ABOMINATIONS** OF EARTH."

Using the definitions of the original terms, let's look at this in language we can understand... **"the woman resides on Satan** (the scarlet beast), **who is full of lies about God's good nature to make Him seem untrustworthy** (names of blasphemy)...**on her forehead her character and nature was written** (name): **A secret or something hidden; through the idea of silence imposed by initiation into religious rites** (mystery). **The spirit that confounds the truth and persecutes is perceived as being in great esteem** (Babylon the Great), **but is in fact the manager of spiritual warfare against us** (mother)..." This would be the prophecy of the Holy Roman Empire, which came into power some 400 years later, as it relates to the concrete story or case study used to teach.

Keyword lookup

Names; Strong's #3686, *onoma* in Greek: the character or nature of something.

Blasphemy; #988, *blasohemia*; vilification of God, rumors or lies about His nature.

Forehead; #3359, *metopon*: the foremind, what occupies the immediate position, your reality.

Mystery; #3466, *musterion*: A secret of hidden things – to impose silence through the idea of religious rites.

Babylon; 897, *babulon*; generically it means to "confound." Here it is used in the context of the spirit of the Holy Roman Empire, the spirit that confounds the truth and persecutes; the most corrupt form of idolatry – *the enemy of true Christians.*

- See page 92 of Thayer's Greek-English Lexicon of the New Testament, copyright 1977 by Baker Book House Company.

Great; 3173, *megas*: the external appearance of things, perceived as "big, important and highly esteemed," while truly being full of arrogance and presumptuous things that are derogatory to the majesty of God.

Mother; 3384, *meter* – manger of the spiritual attack/warfare (city) that produces and harbors the harlots (those who yield themselves to defilement for the sake of personal gain).

Harlots; 4204, *porne* – prostitutes, who yield their souls/selves to defilement for gain (money, power, influence, acceptance, etc.).

Abominations; 946, *bdelugma* – the detestable things and impurities in which we place our trust (false idols).

The **spiritual truth being taught** is about the "foundations of power," and what occurs when institutions or organizations are created with the idea of having power by regulating our beliefs. What occurs is that they sit on top of "the lie" and inadvertently or most certainly they will be the vehicle by which that lie is promoted. This occurred in the Babylonian religions, in the Jewish synagogues, in the pre-Roman Catholic churches, in the Roman Catholic Church, and in the Church of England, and it has spilled into our society at large in attempting to operate apart from God. Today, America's government, institutions, and belief systems are besieged by the serpent, by the spirit of Babylon.

Think if you will about this thing we naively call "the cloud," the Internet out there. How much trust do we put in it? Do we put copies of our personal and private information there? Do we look at information from that collective source as truth? Do we let our children spend hours a day connected to it, getting their minds confused with the untruths and garbage they get fed? Have we grown dependent on it? Google comparisons of America and Babylon and see what you think.

Let's keep going…

Revelation 17:6 reads, "I saw the woman, drunk with the blood of the saints and with the blood of the martyrs on Jesus. And when I saw her, I marveled with great amazement." John was absolutely stunned, astonished, and amazed when he realized that organized religion itself could become a foundation of power enticed by the lie and intoxicated by the bloodshed of those who have truly consecrated themselves to God.

Revelation 17:18 tells John, "And the woman whom you saw is that **city** which **reigns** over the **Kings** of earth". The word *city* (Strong's # 4171/4172) means spiritual warfare, and the word "kings" (Strong's #935) as we know means foundations of power.

I am sure that we can all agree that society pitches false idolatry, i.e. being okay or salvation, through the acquisition of things (status, money, influence, popularity, titles etc.) that give us personal power.

> *"There is a conspiracy of her prophets…they have devoured souls …Her priests have violated my law, and have profaned mine holy things… --Ezekiel 22:25-26 KJV.*

Satan, the spirit of accusation and confusion – the ruler of this world (John 12:31) – the god of this system of things (2 Corinthians 4:4) – the one whose power society is lying in (1 John 5:19) – used his own interpretation of God's words to sell Eve "the lie," and he has continued through society and our systems of thought (institutions, laws, media, movies, video games, etc.) to create confusion and distortion (the spirit of Babylon) about the Truth of God's Word.

A close study of church history will show you that after the first century, the Christ follower movement became something different from what Jesus taught and modeled, and what the Apostles were doing in living by the words of God. It got assimilated into institutionalized religion. As an institution, the church missed Christ's mark, as leaders developed their theological views on the meaning of scripture, made them the agreed-to interpretations by force, and lived by their ways, religious rituals, and traditions. Pictures of an untrustworthy God have been subversively represented through theological misinterpretations.

"Now the Spirit speaketh expressly, that in the later times some shall depart from faith, giving heed to seducing spirits, and doctrine of devils; speaking lies in hypocrisy..." – 1 Timothy 4:1-2

There remains today a fog of deception across society that keeps people from clearly seeing truth. The true church, the body of believers, not Satan, holds the power over human affairs – if we exercise it! Christ delegated to us. He gave us the authority needed to do what seems impossible by worldly standards. Let us not fail to act upon this authority. Join me in studying scripture for spiritual meaning. Let's revive the teachings of Christ in ourselves, and share them with others.

Be a Spell Breaker!

8

THE TEACHINGS OF CHRIST – WHAT'S LOVE GOT TO DO WITH IT?

For those not very familiar with the Bible, bear with me for a page while I address a major misconception about the "nature of love" (God). As a society, I think we really, really just don't get it! The reason for Jesus's sacrifice, emotional torment, torture, and physical death was not to appease an angry, bloodthirsty God who demanded payment for our sins. Jesus is God? It wasn't to reconcile God to us (as the blood atonement theory would have it), but to reconcile us to God. We don't trust God.

Satan's lie, hence our fear, ego and pride (sin), is what stops "us" from believing in God. He has always believed in us. He chose to manifest Himself through human birth, to die in excruciating pain as a man on the cross, and then to rise again in a visible spiritual body to "prove to mankind," the bloodthirsty society, that He can be trusted to "save us" from fear, confusion, heartache, and the self-destructive behaviors of evil, to "prove to us" that what He (God, Christ Jesus) said about who we are was true, because He "loves us" completely. He lived and died as proof that "we" could believe Him. Jesus died for our sins, but not as payment to God (Himself), it was to earn our trust. God loves us enough to go to extreme measures to save us from living in spiritual death, from hell. Humanity chose not to trust and believe in God, and because He is "love," He cannot force us to love back, He cannot impose His will on us to make us believe in Him. Love does not force or demand love back.

God commanded us to love Him with all of our being, because He knows that "if" we do, we will believe Him, not society, and as a result, we will live right lives. If we don't love God, we can't stop sinning, because sinfulness is the result of believing (albeit subconsciously) in the devil's world. It is an either/or situation: there's no way to believe in the lie and the truth at the same time.

God commanded us to love our neighbors (not just our Christian brothers) as ourselves, because we are parts of a larger spiritual body, and "if" we love one another (His kind of love), we won't be willing to hurt others or ourselves with destructive thoughts, words and acts. "Therefore, I command you, Saying, 'you shall open your hand wide to your brother, to your poor and your needy, in your land.'" (Deuteronomy 15:11)

All of our conditions in this world are the result of our thoughts and convictions, "collectively," as humanity. You can't just take care of your immediate family and have harmony in the world, because we are all connected. War won't stop as long as there is a critical mass of humans who believe the "lie." Starvation will not cease until there is a collective selflessness. We have enough food, enough money, and enough resources for all of us to live peaceful lives, but we are greedy because we believe that we have to fend for ourselves. We don't believe that God will provide if we do the right thing; we don't believe that He already provides everything we have.

We think we can get the job, get the girl or guy, and have success in life without Him. We think we can avoid sinful self-destruction without God, and we are wrong.

So what does love have to do with the existence of our species? Absolutely everything! We exist, our beautiful planet exists, and we have each other because of love.

What is love? God is love, which has no limitation, no fear, no doubt, no pride, and contrary to popular belief, no forced demands—just total perseverance, forgiveness, acceptance and grace. Most of us humans, Christians" included, do not understand or operate from this truth.

Let's look at what society understands about love, apart from the Bible. Most people think of love as a personal sentiment that falls somewhere along a wide range of meanings between strong like and loyalty, with the majority of those meanings being self-focused, and not truly expressions of love (God).

We commonly think of love as a "feeling" toward a person or an object. I looked up love in the dictionary, and here's what I found: *strong affection, warm attachment, or attraction based on sexual desire.* ***Love:*** *to value highly or cherish.*

It seems like we could use "love" to describe how we feel about our new jeans, our iPhone, our car, our house, and perhaps our job. We could also use "love" to describe how we feel about our spouse or our children. We do the same thing with the word "belief," sometimes using it to mean "kind of think" or "it's possible," when it was intended to mean we "know" something to be true, without doubt. This creates problems in that we dilute the power and conviction behind two of the most important words in our lives. The importance of the word "love" is lost when used for an object we like. I wouldn't physically die to save my iPhone, while I certainly would to save my son. Also, we mistake love for a "feeling" about something, which is fine for an inanimate object but not for a person.

Love requires action to express itself. I've misunderstood love much of my life, and as a result, sometimes I've been a man of great intentions. I've felt deep love toward people, but these feelings only meant something to me, unless they were expressed with the right actions. I can tell you I love you and mean it, but if I'm not there for you, they might feel like empty words, not real love.

When our love is active, that's when it's real. When I looked up **"loving,"** here's what I found: affectionate, devoted, fond, tender, compassionate, considerate, forgiving, friendly, kind and warmhearted. That's more like it, but it seems like a tall order.

Numerous studies show that a newborn would likely die without human interaction, even in an environment where there is plenty of food, warmth, etc. Right from birth the need for love is so strong that it can affect growth and development, and even bring on death. Look at what we do for love and acceptance in general: as children we either comply to gain adults' approval or act out to get their attention, as a class clown does. As teens we will do almost anything to be accepted within a group (when facing peer pressure). As adults we often dress, look, and talk in ways that the people we want acceptance from do. Then, when dating, we might change ourselves radically to gain the love of the one we love. As a society, we lose touch with our authentic self, chasing love and acceptance.

In Dr. Leo Buscalia's book *Love*, he points out that while love is something we all need, there's not much in the way of classes or instruction on it. We can get law degrees and science degrees, Ph.D.'s in psychology and even theology, but there are no college courses for mastering love. Buscalia rhetorically asks, "Are we born intuitively knowing how to love? Do we assume that it comes to us by way of some mysterious life force? Look at human relationships like marriage, for example. We form promises to be in a lifelong partnership with another person, and yet they have little knowledge." If you wanted to form a successful business, say in an accounting firm, would you look for a partner who had no accounting or consulting knowledge?

Here's what I understand love to be today:

> Not reward for effort... Voluntarily given... Not forced, nor told.
>
> Not in error, nor demanding... but confident and bold.
>
> Never bought, nor sold... but rather true abides in me.
>
> True is commitment... without guarantee.
>
> True is not true, if it asks what can you do for me.
>
> True can only be... as creative expression of thee.
>
> True is active, not passive... It moves about.
>
> It involves dynamic interaction... but you can't fall in, or out.
>
> It's not a state of physical ecstasy, nor disillusionment we're talking about,
>
> But divine true love, without doubt.

Love is unselfish, loyal, and benevolent concern for others, acts of kindness, without thoughts of being loved in return. That doesn't mean I don't want or even hope to have love returned, but if my actions are in any way gauged by what I expect to get back, that's not love; it is trying to love myself (selfishness).

Truth: We live to love and to be loved. We are designed to be expressions of Divine love, that is our function, whether we understand it or not.

If you think you don't agree with me, I challenge you as my brother or sister in humanity to give it some real thought. Be honest with yourself right now as you read this, and think about it. Let yourself feel "your" own truth. What have been the best moments of your life so far? Recall them and visualize them like a movie, if you can. Undoubtedly, they involve experiences of the heart. Were you with someone you loved? Did you really connect? Did you know you mattered? Was someone proud of you? Were you able to express your love for that person and let them know that they mattered? Did you watch someone you loved grow or triumph over an obstacle? Were you part of healing someone's hurt, of helping someone realize a dream? Did you witness someone being totally vulnerable and trusting not be let down, or did those good things happen to you? Were you outdoors in natural beauty or indoors, with music, colors, or visual beauty there? Can you remember eye contact with that beloved person? Did you feel joy for a moment, a feeling of complete and pure happiness for just an instant? Now how much did or do these moments matter? These are literally experiences that account for minutes or hours out of the years of your physical existence, and yet they are so precious. Why?

One last question about your best memories: Do they all involve a relationship, including the one you have with yourself?

How strong is love? Imagine that your brother or sister is about to die. If you could take his or her place, would you? How about your child? Man, I would jump at the chance to swap my life for my son's. If your husband or wife had cancer and you could take on that burden, wouldn't you? What if your biological father rejected or abandoned you, and he died before things were made right? Now imagine all of a sudden he's standing in front of you right now with tears in his eyes, afraid to ask for your forgiveness, but wanting it. Even though he's hurt you, even if you're really good at holding resentments, I bet that you would want to hug him and tell him you love him.

Okay, now be brave and think briefly about your worst moments. What were the most painful impressions? Do they involve the loss of someone you love, the ability to love them, to be loved by them? Did a relationship dissolve, did you let someone down and hurt them, or did they do that to you? Were you abandoned, rejected, or left heartbroken?

Like most people, I have had my heart broken to the degree that life made no sense, and I cannot imagine a physical pain that would feel worse. My point is this: if you are anything like me, your best and your worst moments have been about love, and at the end of it all, it is relationships that matter. Loving other people is really what we are internally driven to do. Most of us do a great job being distracted, busy, and focused on the important responsibilities and goals in life, but the truth is we only engage in these things as a means to the end of living and being loved. It is best if we recognize that and live that way.

In my thoughts, I have always placed a lot of emphasis on love. I was born knowing and being aware that I genuinely love and care about all humans. I hate seeing my fellows suffer, it hurts. That doesn't mean that I've been loving towards all people, because I have "lived in this world," but it does mean that I have felt wrong when my actions haven't lined up with my true heart (my real self). Today, I know when my actions are not expressions of God. In many ways it is easier for me to love strangers than people with whom I have relationships. This is probably because without a relationship, I have no expectations, emotional entanglements, or subconscious motivations about my gestures being returned in some way. The purest love I express is sometimes toward people I do not know. I will always remember one blessed exchange I had with a man named Tom, who was homeless. He was outside Starbucks asking for change and his focus was on another person as I went in, but I caught his dejected look as someone coldly ignored him. I found myself watching him while I was in line. I saw deep sadness and shame in his eyes as someone put money in his cup, and that made my heart hurt. I didn't give any conscious thought to approaching him, other than that I would put five bucks in his cup. I was unemployed myself and only had twenty-five dollars, so I rationalized giving him the lesser of the two bills. He looked like he hadn't showered or worn clean clothes in a long time. There was visible dirt on his face, forearms, and hands, and the odor that accompanied his look was as expected. I walked up and put the money in his cup before he could say anything to me. He smiled with surprise. I nodded and kept walking. As I took a few steps he said in what sounded like a genuine tone of voice, "God bless you," which stopped me in my tracks. I turned around to tell him the same "God bless you, too!" and instinctively I reached out my hand, saying "I'm John." He shook my hand and replied with his name, Tom. As our eyes met, his started to fill with tears and his lips quivered as he spoke, "Thank you, John. Thanks for the money, and thank you for 'seeing' me." At first, I thought he meant "seeing" that there was a guy with a cup who needed money, but that's not what he meant. He was thanking me for seeing him as a human being, worthy of love from a fellow human. Tom then proceeded to tell me that most people don't make eye contact with him, they look down or away as if he doesn't exist, even when they put money in his cup. He said that when I shook his filthy hand it was the first time someone had physically touched him in over a year, and that gesture meant more to him than I could know. We talked for a minute or so and I told him that we're all one step away from homelessness (I actually was), to keep his head up, and that it was my pleasure to have met him.

As we parted, much to my surprise, the words, "Love you, brother," came out of my mouth. I wasn't a Christian at this point in life, and I had never read the Bible, but I had always thought of God as being the essence of love and had the suspicion that when things like this happened, it was God's love occurring, not mine. Years later, as a Christian, I understand this to be true; unselfish love is an expression of God. Imagine being in Tom's situation and knowing that you are alone in the world, that there isn't one person with whom you have a relationship, no one is waiting to see you, to talk to you. There's no one and no place to go "home" to. You have not a soul to share life with. Imagine never being hugged again or told that you are loved, imagine not mattering. It is really sad.

What would happen if each of us talked to just one stranger a day who looked in need of contact? Or what if we took it a step further and actually smiled, made eye contact, and said "Hello" or "Have a good day" to as many people as we encountered? I wonder if we did flash mobs of loving kindness, what that would be like? We get so caught up, so preoccupied and focused on our own little world that sometimes we don't see those with whom we are sharing the world.

Try and experiment tomorrow an reach out to people all day long with a hello, a smile, or wishes for a good day, and notice what happens. Watch people's reaction: their body language will change with improved posture, an extra bounce in their step, or a wide smile. Then notice the effect on you. By the end of the day, even though you've been projecting love all day, you will be more filled with love than when you started. This is how the soul works.

James Twyman said it well, "The ego seeks its own comfort, accumulating goods and money in the fruitless attempt to ward off death… The soul, on the other hand, seeks to give as much as possible, because it knows that it isn't limited by separation or death, and it can only realize this through giving away what it most desires." You can't give what you don't have. The sinner in us (our ego) wants to get, while the Christ in us (the soul) wants to give. We only experience true happiness or joy when our soul is giving (loving). While it is our nature to express God's love, that is not "natural" for us, while living in this world of deception. In order to love like Christ Jesus, we have to think like Christ Jesus.

> *And do not be conformed to this world, but be transformed by the renewing of your mind, that you may prove what is that good and acceptable and perfect will of God.* (Romans 12:2)

The taming of our egos won't happen simply because we intellectually agree with any of this. It really is spiritual warfare, and our part in the battle is to rid ourselves of the practical routine of living without Christ.

Love is unselfish. You can't insist that someone you love has to love you back. Love comes of free will. If a woman complains to her man that he never buys her flowers, and he rolls his eyes, then brings her some flowers the next day and gives them to her saying, "Are you satisfied now?," I'll bet she won't feel loved.

Erich Fromm said, "Love is an act of faith, and whoever is of little faith is of little love."

We are taught from childhood to expect reward for effort, but it does not work that way with love. In fact, some people are incapable of really accepting love, much less returning it, so no matter how hard you try, how much effort you put in, or how many sacrifices you make, that person may not love you back.

We have all felt the pain and heartache of rejection. In fact, I don't think it is possible to have relationships without being let down.

Key: Love has the power to build a child up into a confident, balanced person, while lack of love, rejection, and abandonment will leave people insecure and seeking validation in unhealthy ways from unhealthy people.

All the stuff we've discussed so far about "the lie" is connected to love. We feel separated, apart, and alone. We long for togetherness, connectedness, and union. We live under the deception that we are not loved by God. Look around at people with troubled lives, addiction, co-dependency, depression, adultery, obesity, anorexia, at people who get plastic surgery to look more loveable, at people who chase money and think that if they are rich they will be loved, at heroes who save the day so that they will be loved, and at teens who get drunk and have casual sex while secretly hoping to find true love.

Actually, the list goes on and on, and includes all of us. Almost all of our motivations, good and bad, selfish and giving, are tied to our need to express and share love.

There's nothing wrong with wanting to love and wanting to be loved. **It is what we are designed to do as physical expressions of God. It is actually what we (our real selves) are, as God's image and likeness**. It is very, very difficult, however, to get the unconditional love and acceptance that we long for from each other, because we all end up forming expectations and having our own wants and needs in return. There is only one place where we can find the unconditional validation and security we "all" seek, and that our souls thirst for, and that is from God, Christ Jesus.

Accepting His love, losing separateness, surrendering our wills, fears, and anxieties to His protection, guidance and care, there in His arms we see that we are loved, that we (our real selves) are perfect, that we are desired, valued and cherished. When we can accept this and feel it, then we have it to give to others. No longer do you "need" validation that you are worthy. With confidence, you know that you are special and important. The perfect thing is that when you believe this, all of a sudden you are free to focus your love on others: you have it to give, and you don't need to get love back in return. And because your love is real, confident, and bold, you are extremely loveable. It is a self-fulfilling prophecy: accept God's love, love others like He loves, and be surrounded by love.

Truly, I say to you, the Bible contains the master curriculum on love, from elementary school through Ph.D. levels. Like all schools, you need to be a student and follow the instructions to learn, develop, and advance. I'm not talking about just a book you read, but the text you study over years, the words that come to life, the encounters with Jesus, the conversations you personally have with the Holy Spirit, the refining of your heart (mind), the place where you go to connect with God, and so much more.

In the original Biblical manuscripts, which were written in the Hebrew, Aramaic, and Greek languages, there are several different words used to express the various aspects of love, such as romantic love, soul love, loyal love, self-sacrificial love, brotherly love, family love, etc. As the Old Testament and New Testament were translated into the English language, most of those descriptive words were folded into our generic word "love," which is why the modern meaning of "love" is so loosely defined. But more to the point, the Bible teaches very specifically how to love in different situations and relationships. It covers loving God, your wife or husband, your children, your friends, your fellow believers, your community and strangers, your enemies, and yourself.

The Bible teaches about healthy, non-codependent love, selfless motivations, forgiveness, "remaining in" love during conflict, or while dealing with disappointment, heartache, injustice, and tragedy. It teaches about responsible love and how to accept, share, and give love. I could go on and on, but I think you get the point. It truly teaches all about love.

Big Picture: You are either living out your existence in the physical realm as your authentic self, an ethereal-spiritual being, your soul a reflection and expression of **love** (God) OR your physical body is literally living as an imposter (in the flesh), as an expression of **fear** (the evil idea of Satan), to which the soul is susceptible. We will look at the concept of spiritual warfare in more depth, but a little thought about this will strengthen your understanding of the teachings on love as we go through them. Think of it this way: your physical host, earthen vessel, or suit, as I have called it, is either inhabited by God, in which case the real you (your ethereal body, spiritual self, or soul) **expands** to integrate, permeate, and blend into the host, or it **contracts**, in which case a demonic spirit takes advantage of the opportunity to enter and coinhabits the physical host (via thoughts). Love expands the soul, while fear contracts it.

Truth: God's purpose for you and me, His heart's desire (will), is for us to express love and His concept of love, that's it! When we listen to, hear, and heed (obey) His instructions (commands) to love Him with all of our being and to love our neighbors (fellow souls) as "ourselves," as authentic reflections of God who love as He does, we are being expressions of Divine love—that is what God's commands are—to express his love in the world.

One of my favorite published prayers, written by St. Francis of Assisi, which by the way I first read in the Alcoholics Anonymous book, "*Twelve Steps and Twelve Traditions*," is asking God to use us to express love, "Lord make me a channel of thy peace—that where there is hatred, I may bring the spirit of forgiveness—that where is discord, I may bring harmony—that where there is error, I may bring truth—that where there is doubt, I may bring faith—that where there is despair, I may bring hope—that where there are shadows, I may bring light—that where there is sadness, I may bring joy. Lord, grant that I may seek rather to comfort than to be comforted—to understand, than to be understood—to love, than to be loved. For it is by self-forgetting that one finds. It is by forgiving that one is forgiven. It is by dying that one awakens to Eternal Life. Amen."

There are several aspects of divine love. There's creative love from which the miracles of child conception and birth occurs, there's loyal love, where triangular commitment between Christ and two people overcomes selfishness, there's soul love, in which our selves see each other and form a bond, and there's selfless love in general (agape), where the soul seeks to give, not just emotionally, but in acts of kindness, hospitality, and charity to strangers. The traits of divine love, as our spiritual gift, are described in 1 Corinthians 13:

> "If I speak in tongues of men and of angels, but have no love, I am a noisy gong or clanging cymbal. And if

> I have prophetic powers, and understand all mysteries and all knowledge, and if I have faith as to remove mountains, but have not love, I am nothing. If I give away all I have, and if I deliver up my body to be burned, but have not love, I gain nothing. Love is patient and kind; love does not envy or boast; it is not arrogant or rude. It does not insist on its own way; it is not irritable or resentful; it does not rejoice at wrongdoing, but rejoices with the truth. Love bears all things, believes all things, hopes all away; as for tongues, they will cease; as for knowledge, it will pass away. For we know now in part and we prophesy in part, but when that which is perfect has come, then that which is in part will be done away. When I was a child, I reasoned like a child. When I became a man, I gave up childish ways. For now we see in the mirror dimly, but the face-to-face. Now that I know in part, then I shall know fully, even as I have been fully known. So now faith, hope, and love abide, these three; but the greatest of these is love."

If two people loved each other this way, they would surely conquer all problems.

Classes on Love: So, in the Bible we learn about the Divine Creator's nature as Love, and about ours as a species whose intended purpose is to live as expressions of that Love.

There are classes on the "Characteristics and Aspects of Love," in the books First Corinthians, (as just read), Philippians, and Romans, where we can learn what constitutes love, what it is and its characteristics. There's instruction on the "Loyalty of Love" in Samuel. We learn what genuine friendship is through how Jonathan loves his friend David. Then in Ruth we learn more about the binding loyalty of love (real love) in the context of marriage, when after her husband dies she stays with her mother-in-law in a foreign land, under adverse conditions, out of loyalty to her heart and the triangular covenant she made with God and her husband. Throughout the four Gospels and the New Testament there is a series of higher education tracts on responsible love for every type of relationship we have: with spouses, family, extended family, friends and community, with strangers and enemies, and then our relationship with God.

Let's take a closer look at these relationship types, starting with "romantic," and using scripture as the authority on "how to." Note that for every example of scripture I will use, there are numerous others expanding, reinforcing, and detailing just what love is, how to cultivate it, and how to express it.

It is one of the most amazing and sacred gifts when we get a glimpse of another soul. Outside of my romantic connections, there are only a small number of people whose souls I have been blessed to see: my son's, my close friends Marvin, Ted, and Bobby's, several immediate family members, and a few others. Each holds a special place in my heart (mind), and I carry them with me. I might not get to see some of them for a number of years, but I always feel connected to them and trust that our bond will transcend all obstacles. In a manner of speaking, once you connect with another soul and form a bond, they abide within you and you within them (they live in your mind). An imprint or impression of them (their soul) is stamped on you (your soul).

Romantic Love: Romantic connections are more complex and confusing, it seems. We have all kinds of notions about it, from having a crush, to a torrid affair, to finding our "soulmate." The quest for romance is surely exciting, but it can also be the most destructive and misguided form of idolatry in our lives. By this I mean we can unwittingly cast our hope and trust onto the notion that in this special relationship we will find security, that everything will fall into place, or that we will be complete, thus placing our trust in a false salvation. Ideally, one would be secure and complete before joining is this kind of partnership. Ideally, one would already have an established spiritual life.

The sometimes subconscious drive to find a life partner feels primal—the need for connection, companionship, affection, and physical touch is real; it is a primary way that the soul (your real self) validates its existence. This kind of union between two souls is divinely designed, and has a deeper purpose than many of us realize. The soul is constantly seeking to reconcile with the physical ego, to exist in the world (our conscious thought). Have you ever heard someone make reference to their romantic partner as "completing them," or "feeling home" when near that person? That's because when your soul truly connects with another soul, it realizes itself in the physical realm; when you have that connection, it validates the truth of who you are (the inner-person).

The physiological experience of a kiss is amazing, and two bodies coming together as God designed them to is wondrous and spiritual—but there is a huge difference between that and just sex, where there is attraction, "lust," and physical pleasure—versus God's design of spiritual and physical attraction, "love," sexual and soul pleasure, creative beauty and joy—as two people emanate the spiritual expression of love from their true selves towards each other in an effort to connect and blend (really making love), which is divine.

The exchange is very different, however, when one or both people are not in touch with motives of love; if one person is purely seeking a casual encounter, while the other is attempting to connect; one person is more consciously aware of, or in touch with their inner self, while the other soul is more guarded or fearful. Having sex without an actual mutual connection can bring confusion because there's the potential for the illusion of a bond. In other words, you have sex with the "imposter," and don't connect with the real-person (spiritual being). That experience can leave us feeling empty, guilty, and a little dumbfounded, and can subconsciously damage the soul, which is left with fear.

God's design for romantic love, marriage, is meant to be a committed and triangular union between the individual souls who have been drawn to, seen, and connected with each other, and the Spirit from which they exist (God). In such a union they are supporting each other as soulmates, and when they look at each other, touch each other, and fall asleep next to each other, they are bringing their souls into the conscious realm.

Peter Marshall, the famed preacher who became the chaplain to the U.S. Senate, captured the spirit of this union well: "It is fusion of two hearts—union of two lives—the coming together of tributaries, which, after being joined in marriage, will flow in the same channel in the same direction…" "The perfect marriage must be a blend of the spiritual, the physical, the social, and the intellectual… We are souls living in bodies. Therefore when we **REALLY** fall in love, it isn't just physical attraction. If it's just that, it won't last. Ideally, it's also a spiritual attraction. God has opened our eyes and let us see into someone's soul. We have fallen in love with their inner person, the person who's going to live forever. That's why God is the greatest asset to romance. He thought it up in the first place. Include Him in every part of your marriage and He will lift it above the level of mundane to something rare, beautiful, and lasting.

Maybe this is why the Bible teaches about monogamy, not to be controlling or oppressive, not to limit our freedom, but for our sanity and the sake of our soul.

Two souls awakening to this union, following God together, will project love beyond themselves to their children, their community and into the world. They will create and raise people who bring their spiritual selves into the conscious reality which they make. The cascading effect of an army of families like this could bring love and peace to society. Conversely, people repeatedly engaging in purely casual sex are at best self-medicating the pain of not finding themselves, and at worst, corrupting each other into a state of mental numbness, being further lost souls, contracting from fear and making room for Satan's influence on their physical beings.

A Class on God's Design for Romantic Love: It may be a surprise to many people, but the Bible actually teaches about romantic soulmate love, what marriage is meant to be, and what's required to make it last. It describes being "in love," the lovesick, euphoric stuff and "soulmates." It teaches about sex as a beautiful and meaningful expression of love, how to be intimate, passionate lovers, and about the friendship, kinship, and loyalty between soulmates, and the sacrifice and hard work that a marriage entails.

The Song of Solomon is a book in the Bible that provides us with an understanding of God's design for marriage. It's a romantic love story between a country girl and the King, and celebrates the importance of sexuality as a part of the full experience of humanity in the context of a Godly marriage. Through poetry, the lovers express their deep passion and longing for each other, and demonstrate the intimacy and beauty of human love that can exist in married life. *The Song of Solomon* teaches that a marriage requires physical, emotional, and spiritual passion, dedication, commitment, and strong loyalty.

As I mentioned before, the English translation of the Bible uses the one word "love" in place of the many different words and expressions used in the original manuscripts.

In *The Song of Solomon*, there were originally numerous Hebrew words and expressions used to articulate different aspects or expressions of romantic love, making it a bit difficult for the average casual reader to get a succinct understanding. I will point out some of those as we look at what is being taught. Examples of the original word expressions are: "sexual love," "dear companion," "self-sacrificing love," "sexual longing," "sexual passion," "erotic love," "spouse," "lover," and "sexual completion."

NOTE: Much of the Bible really requires study, not only because of the potential loss of preciseness in language translation, but also because much of it is written as poetry, which relies on the ancient symbolism of the Middle East (what is modern-day Iraq, for example). Comprehension is not simply a matter of taking things literally or metaphorically, but of understanding what type of writing you are reading, the context, etc.

A couple of notes about this *Book of Solomon* before we walk through the chapters.

- It was written in the Middle Eastern culture in the literary form of an idyll (a type of love song). Think of it as a musical play where the lyrics are in poetry. The story is told by the two main characters, King Solomon and his bride, with others singing the chorus as transitions from one scene to the next, not necessarily in chronological order, but as vignettes.
- At the time of Jesus's birth, Jewish scholars took this scripture as allegorically describing the love of God for Israel. Similarly, some Christians teach that the book speaks of the love between Christ and His bride, the church. While I personally can relate to applying the kind of passion, intensity, and commitment described in some specific verses to my relationship with Christ, one need not look into allegorical meaning to understand the Song. It clearly celebrates the beauty and intimacy (spiritual, emotional, sexual) of love

> within a human marriage in a poem. If it was about God, we would have to ask what the lengthy, graphic, and erotic narrative on human sexuality has to do with theology.

Awareness of the different Hebrew words that were replaced by "love" in the English translation brings light to where the book says things like "love-making," sexual embrace," "sexual completion," or "awakened sexually," and knowing that "apple trees," "raisin cakes" and "fruits" are symbols for sexual passion in ancient love songs, and bring expanded color to the sexual lovemaking described, but even a novice reader with a plain English Bible (rather than a study Bible with notes and references) would have a really hard time denying what they are reading about.

The husband talks with passion and longing about her body parts: "breasts," "the shape of her thighs," her "lips," "mouth," "waist," "navel," and "neck." And she describes the most intimate part of her anatomy with words like "garden," "fountain" and "honeycomb." Just as they are about to make love for the first time on their wedding night in the King's bed, she says to him, "Blow on my garden, that its spices may flow out," and "Let my beloved come to his garden and eat its fruits," and after they make love he says, "I went down to the garden…" and then proceeds to state his satisfaction. We are talking about human sexuality as a bonding expression of their love (becoming one flesh), and I really don't see how that is twisted into a theological analogy involving God and us.

The *Song of Solomon* opens with the young bride telling her girlfriends about how great her sex life with her husband is: "Let him kiss me with his mouth—For your love (the Hebrew noun used here means sexual love) is better than wine…" and then she and her friends go back and forth about how handsome he is, what a great catch he is, and how in love they are. In verse seven, the bride speaks to her husband, "Tell me O you whom I love (the literal rendering here is, "whom my soul or inner being loves"), then she goes on to tell him her fears that he will be too busy with his kingdom work for them to spend lots of time together, and how much she desires to be his true companion (best friend and partner).

In verse fifteen, the husband tells her how beautiful she is, and that she is his best friend, "Behold, you are air (beautiful), my love! (the Hebrew for love used here means "dear companion.") You have dove's eyes (symbolizing purity, innocence, and beauty). She then responds, telling him how handsome he is, and how she desires him. In Chapter Two, the couple go back and forth talking about their mutual passion for each other. Then the bride pauses to tell her girlfriends how self-sacrificing he is towards her and how loved she feels; she then cautions her friends to maintain sexual purity so they can experience this type of special divine bond that she and her husband have.

Chapter Four is the husband professing his adoration for her, verbally making love to her, telling her in detail how every part of her body is perfect to him, describing her features as "wonderful," "sexually attractive" and "desirable," "sexy," "fun," "graceful," "special," "delightful," etc. Then he tells her just how much it means, how much he treasures the fact that he will be her first and only sexual partner, that they will have shared themselves only with each other. They dialogue back and forth as they prepare to make love for the first time, and she tells him that she's ready, "Awake O north wind, And come, O south, Blow upon my garden, That its spices may flow out. Let my beloved come to his garden, and eat its pleasant fruits.

Chapter Five opens at the conclusion of the couple's lovemaking and the husband telling her how satisfied he is with her. The rest of the chapter is the bride recounting a bad dream to her girlfriends in which she can't find her husband. Then in six, she tells him about her fears related to the dream and his being gone, and he reassures her that they belong to each other, and continues to tell her how much he cherishes her.

Chapter seven gets a little steamy as Solomon rhapsodizes on her beauty and his desire to get her pregnant. In his eyes, his lover has a beauty that transcends what others might see. He talks about the curves of her thighs, her breasts, and his longing to be with her.

Verses 6 to 9: "How fair (beautiful) and pleasant you are, O love (the Hebrew noun used is 'self-sacrificial love'), with your delights! This stature of yours is like a palm tree, And your breasts like clusters. I said, 'I will go up to the palm tree, Let now your breasts be clusters of the vine, The fragrance of your breath like apples, And the roof of your mouth like the best wine."

Note from the New King James Study Bible on this verse:

"Palm tree: This is a sexual image that has its basis in the pollination of Palm trees. To fertilize a female palm tree, the gardener climbs the male tree and takes some of its flowers. Then he climbs the female tree. The gardener climbs the female tree and ties pollen-bearing flowers among its branches."

In the final chapter, the bride tells her husband that she feels she has known him for her entire life, and talks about the joys of the total intimacy in their marriage, pausing to warn her girlfriends again against sexual activity before marriage.

In my mind, verses six and seven are up there with the most powerfully romantic phrases of all time—as she articulates her total and undying commitment to him—he has all of her and she is committed to only him, wanting him to be completely committed to her. As long as she resides in his heart, she feels secure. She knows that deeply-rooted love is intense (strong as death) and passionate (flames of fire), and that true love cannot be destroyed nor purchased (quenched… despised).

Verse Six: "Set me as a seal upon your heart, As a seal upon your arm; For love is as strong as death, Jealousy as cruel as the grave; Its flames are flames of fire, A most vehement flame."

Verse Seven: "Many waters cannot quench love, Nor can the floods drown it. If a man would give for love all the wealth of his house, it would be utterly despised."

These verses are perhaps the place where I can most clearly see the application to that of my relationship with Christ. In fact, when I read these words (or listen to my favorite Jesus culture song based on them), I am gripped and deeply emotional about the seal on my heart to Christ, and my thoughts are about Him. Secondarily, in the context of marriage, I can see that love then being extended to include my soulmate in a triangle, the divinely blessed union.

It ends with the bride's brothers talking about how she came from a fatherless home, and how protective they were of her virtue; her talking about how virtuous she was throughout her youth, and how faithful she will remain to her husband, saying that in her divine union she is "sexually complete."

Then she talks to her husband, telling him how dedicated she is to him, and it closes with the bride sharing a story with her girlfriends of how one time before their marriage she had told him to go away in order to protect her virginity and their purity, because she was getting too aroused.

Typically, we don't find too much teaching at church about the intimacy and sexual expression found in the Bible, I think for good reason. My point in looking at *The Song of Solomon* with you was simply to demonstrate the breadth and completeness of the Bible's instruction on love.

It is not easy for couples to keep God at the center of their marriage and family. At least, it was a struggle in my marriage, but when it is done, when we are willing to override fears and selfish wants to heed

God's will and put our faith in Him, it is an amazingly beautiful expression of loyal love.

Before we move on, I want to share a story with you, the story of Sabina and Richard Wumbrand, a married Christian couple living in Communist Romania in the 1940s-1950s.

Richard was a Christian Pastor. They had one biological son, and adopted six other orphan children. One Sunday morning, February 29th, 1948, Richard left for church ahead of his family to perform a marriage, telling his wife, "See you there." He never made it. For several weeks, Sabina frantically searched for any information about her husband, checking with hospitals, police, friends and neighbors, praying that he was alive.

She was a stay-at-home mother, but now needed to work to provide for her son and herself. In order to work at that time in Communist Romania, you needed what was called a 'ration card.' Without it, you could not work or buy food.

When Sabina applied the card and was rejected, the authorities told her it was because her husband had been arrested as a traitor of sorts. They wouldn't tell her where he was, but said the government had taken him from the local authorities, and as the wife of a traitor, she could not work. They told her that if she was willing to divorce him, they would let her back into their good graces, but she refused. This was a tactic frequently used by the Communists to try and break the spirit of Christian prisoners, hoping that it would cause a turn away from faith. She continued to refuse to divorce him, so they arrested her, and she spent several years in prison labor camps under extremely harsh conditions.

When Sabina was released from prison, she was reunited with her son, and over time a dear friend, another man, started helping her and her son. She needed money, food, companionship and someone to help raise her son, and started to fall in love with this man. She spoke to another pastor about her situation, and he advised her to never see this man again.

Scripture teaches to not commit adultery in the heart by even thinking about being with another man, and that divorce, "breaking the covenant made with God and her husband," is something to be avoided. Satan uses fear and loneliness as footholds to get into your mind and weaken resolve and faith to stay selfless. Sabina did the hard thing and never saw that man again, even as a friend. Two weeks later, out of the blue, she got a postcard from her husband that said, "Time and distance quench a small love, but make a great love grow stronger." Prisoners were allowed to write one 15-word postcard each year. That was the first time she had heard from him in five years. This was God's intervention. Now that she knew where he was, she tried to visit him, but was not allowed to do so. Her son was able to visit his father one Christmas, though.

Then, one afternoon in 1956, eight years after he was taken, he showed up on the porch. She had not had companionship, sex, or help from her husband in eight years, never committed adultery physically or by divorce. As a result, her son had his father and mother again, she had the husband she was still very much in love with, and their marriage was still blessed by God.

A few years later, he was arrested again for being Christian. Through Sabina's tireless efforts to find help and a Christian humanitarian organization, in 1965 she was able to ransom her husband back for $10,000.

This family's life was filled with difficult trials and temptations, but never did either Richard or Sabina surrender their faith. If not for her loyal love and this faith and loyalty to Christ, Richard would have died in prison.

Instead, their son had his parents alive, and they had each other into old age as best friends, as one. They both ministered and taught the gospel to many people in and out of prison, and started an organization to help other persecuted Christians, "Voice of the Martyrs," which has helped to free many people who were falsely imprisoned under similar situations, saving many lives.

As we get into the other types of love taught in the Bible, our order of importance might logically be to look at love of family next, then friends and loving other believers, followed by loving God, then neighbors (strangers), and lastly, love of enemies—going from most to least in terms of personal sentiment. However, Jesus's teachings on love had less to do with family and friends, and more to do with a call to an impersonal but active love for our entire species, and a deeply personal love between Him and us.

There is certainly plenty of instruction in the Bible on loving those we have personal relationships with, and even though we may not "love them well," as a society that's where we place our emphasis. With all of this in mind, we are going to place the importance on teaching love for our enemies and strangers, on the theology of Christ, then God's love for us and ours for Him, then friends and family.

I yearn for humanity to "truly love," and I frequently pray about that for all of us as the apostle Paul did, "For God as my witness, how I yearn for you all, with the affection of Christ Jesus. And it is my prayer, that your love may abound more and more with knowledge and discernment." (Philippians 1:8-9).

The Theology of Christ: It probably makes sense to do a quick level set of the theology that Christ (God) taught because He rejected, challenged, and debunked the Old World notion of God's nature and character, along with the delusional assumptions and repressive values from which religious men were operating. Many of those remain intact today in the common "Christian" worldview.

The early Apostles and Disciples understood Jesus' teaching, but with the embracing of Christianity by the Roman Empire came again the pattern of misappropriation of language, symbols and Scripture, subversively diluting and changing the message and theology of Christ.

Heresy is not questioning what men teach each other about our understanding of scripture's meaning. Heresy is preaching anything that does not conform to the teachings or nature of Christ.

Belonging to, and participating in a local church, and living in true Christian community with those people, is extremely important, but our allegiance must remain to Christ and His body (the true Church), not to any man-governed organization lest it divert us from our purpose.

His theology: Jesus envisioned the world transformed through our actions, through our expression of His love, a world where people, powers, and the Creator lived in harmony — the "Kingdom of God." He rejected domination, violence, oppression, and favoritism. He taught against selfishness, lying, cheating, and stealing; against the marginalizing of individuals or groups, against separatism and exclusion. His teachings and instructions were about responsible love, about caring for those lacking the resources to provide for their own basic needs, the poor, the sick, the disabled, the lepers, the blind, the insane, and the refugees. He taught that we could stop people from turning to stealing, prostitution, or forms of bondage to survive by sharing and helping. He made it perfectly clear that God did not favor a race, gender, or socio-economic status. He taught that we are all family, and that true repentance and reconciliation was what we should drive each other towards, not through evil force, but through real love. He asked that we follow Him in becoming willing to put down this physical life in favor of the true spiritual and eternal one, rather than living under the deception of fallen angels and committing evil.

NOTE: In the West, we tend to forget that Jesus and

Christianity came from the Middle East. Abraham was born in the location that is known today as Baghdad, Iraq. Turkey, Syria, and Greece were major areas where Paul planted the early Christian churches. Jesus wasn't from a pure Jewish lineage.

In just about every encounter Jesus has in the Bible, He's violating the religious and social customs of the time, indicting the existing powers as evil. For example, Jewish men were not allowed to speak to women in public, but Jesus did. He took sides with a prostitute who later became an Apostle, and He referred to an old, poor, uneducated, lower-class woman as the "daughter of Abraham," giving her full status as a holy person. Women were not subjugated in Christ's presence, they were Apostles. (Romans 16:7) and Disciples (Acts 9:36-42), and led churches (Philemon 1-2). They were truly equals. Another example would be Jesus healing a man on the Sabbath, much to the chagrin of the religious men in the community. And the list goes on.

The Catholic Church today does not have anything close to the influence and power that it did decades ago. Hence, it is not directly responsible for violent acts at this point. The Christian denominations operate more as local churches without too much hierarchical structure. As a result, the instruction of Jesus is more closely taught today than, say, two centuries ago. But I wonder what would happen if say, the Pope, all Cardinals, Bishops, their Priests and parishes, along with all of the local Christian (non-Catholic) churches across the world did a mass "sit-in" and call for non-violence. What if every "Christian" man decided to really have faith in Christ and followed His direction, refusing to kill another person, refusing to fight in the military anywhere, at all costs—as Christ modeled?

How long would it take for soldiers of opposing forces, say Muslims or Communists, to buckle to humanity and love? How long could they stay hateful and violent if we all were truly loving? How many individual consciences could resist love in favor of hate? How many would join Christ's followers and receive Salvation? Jesus told us to find out. Fallen angels tell us not to trust Jesus. Who are we all listening to today, the Father, or the rebellious angels?

Can you imagine how much power there would be for positive change "if" we actually were willing to follow Jesus's teaching, if we "truly" believed, if we really were willing to forsake ourselves and this worldly physical life for one where we let love and spirituality guide us, not fear?

What if the same body of believers brought all of their possessions together, even at a neighborhood or city-by-city level, pooling resources to care for each other, for the needy—as Jesus pleaded with us to do? What would happen to crime? How would this change the hardened hearts of both those who have and those who have not? No war and sharing what we have. I know these are radical, even irrational-sounding thoughts. My point is simply that these are the things God, in the Bible, asks us to do.

We can look at two of the more popular spiritual teachings of Jesus, the "Beatitudes" and the "Lord's Prayer," and see Christ's complete system of theology, where we are all family seeking God's kingdom, where violence and domination are rejected, and where the spiritual development of our souls is taught.

The Beatitudes: Jesus knew that we are fallen man in a constant state of spiritual warfare. He understood that our egos believe and actually perpetuate the "lie," that we think we are our own makers, our own gods. So He shared the spiritual truth about "humility," which is that it is key to opening the door to faith.

Truth: We are personally powerless and will create a sinful mess of our lives and the planet if left to our own devices without the help of God; however, our egos fight against this. Few of us will actually seek God and then become willing to turn our lives over to His care until we accept that we alone cannot manage our lives until we admit our own powerlessness, until we are at a place of true humility.

"Blessed (fortunate) are "the poor," "the hungry," "the sad" (those who are in spiritual poverty)… because they are stripped of false pride and will become willing to turn to God. When you "hit bottom," so to speak, when your best efforts have failed, when you are poor and have no food, when you are filled with sorrow, when your ego is small enough to turn in desperation to a Power greater than yourself.

"Blessed are you poor, For yours is the kingdom of God.

Blessed are you who hunger now, For you shall be filled.

Blessed are you who weep now, For you shall laugh…"

Conversely, "woe to those" who have financial wealth, material comfort, and security, because you think you have everything you need, you think you have it all under control, you believe you are self-sufficient, you believe "the lie." You are filled with pride, arrogance, and ego-separation from God. Your "self-will" brings you much suffering and heartache yet, until it takes you to your knees.

> "But woe to you who are rich, For you have received your consolation. Woe to you who are full, For you shall hunger. Woe to you who laugh now, For you shall morn and weep…" –Matthew 5:1-10, also Luke 6:20-26, New King James Version

When Jesus was asked how to pray, He responded with this carefully constructed prayer, which when analyzed, contains the whole message of Christ, and by design provides continued spiritual development of the soul each time it is prayed.

There are seven clauses and an affirmation. In the Bible, seven symbolizes individual completeness and perfection of the soul, while twelve represents corporate completeness.

The Lord's Prayer:

"Our Father, which art in heaven, Hallowed be thy name. Thy kingdom come. Thy will be done, on earth as it is in heaven. Give us this day our daily bread. And forgive us our trespasses, As we forgive them that trespass against us. And lead us not into temptation; But deliver us from evil; For thine is the kingdom, the power, and the glory, Forever and ever." –Matthew 6:5+, also Luke 11:2-4

The opening statement tells us about the truth of Being, about the nature and character of God, about ourselves and our neighbors. "Our Father" indicates a parent-child relationship where we can expect care, guidance, and protection. It also indicates that as offspring, we are similar in nature. We are essentially divine spirits, too.

Notice it is "Our" Father, not "my" Father, telling us that we are all His children, that our fellow humans are our siblings. There is no favoritism, no preferred race, etc.

"Which art in Heaven" - While we are not separated from God, we are not one and the same. The parent-child relationship makes clear different functions here. We see that God is in heaven and man is on earth. Heaven is the presence of God, the realm of pure ideas, while Earth is the manifestation, the physical realm. Our Father is the Cause, and we are meant to express that cause on the physical plane. When we attempt to express without the Cause (atheism, materialism) we have diverted from our harmonious purpose. We become fallen man.

"Hallowed be thy name" - Name is the essential nature of something, its character. Hallowed, meaning holy, wholesome, healed, etc. "Hallowed be thy name" means "His nature is altogether good." According to scripture, this means that God cannot send us sickness, trouble, death, etc.: "the same fountain cannot send forth bitter and sweet water."

Thy kingdom come, Thy will be done, on earth as it is in heaven" - This means it is our duty to be occupied in helping to establish the kingdom of God on earth, (not just waiting for the day when it comes!). Being the expression of God means to express in concrete, the abstract ideas from God. We need His creative power to do this, which will come intuitively through prayer. Each of us is an individualized consciousness of God, distinct but not separate. Each has a unique role which God planned for us, **an active role, not a passive one**.

"Give us this day our daily bread" - The message here is total dependence. We can expect God our Father to provide everything we need spiritually and physically: direction, food, shelter, money, and people to share love with. He is the source, not us, not our ego, AND He provides it on a "daily" basis. We need daily conscious contact with God, an ongoing contact where all of our decisions and activities arise through this contact and God's will for us (heart's desire). There is no need for greed or coveting. You can freely share your resources because He will replenish them. If you seek a secondary source, "self-will," it will fail. If you view your job as the source, what happens when you lose your job? If you believe, pray to God and trust. He will open the door to a new channel when one closes.

"Forgive us our trespasses, as we forgive them that trespass against us" - Our true selves are undivided from God, expressing His ideas, witnessing His nature—the thinking of His mind. Evil, sin, and the fall of man are the attempts of our ego to know the truth.

We forgive others and ourselves, knowing that setting others free means freeing ourselves, and we seek forgiveness from God, those we harm and ourselves, we accept forgiveness as love; reconciliation, harmony, and peace are the Truth of our being.

"Lead us not into temptation, but deliver us from evil" - This makes reference to the subtle difficulties that spring up from spiritual pride, self-righteousness, temptations to work for self-glory or personal gain. "I've got this," we tell ourselves as we relapse into forgetting our dependence on God and losing our daily conscious contact with our Higher Power. Then, ceasing to seek His heart's desire (will) for us, we attempt to take control and manage our lives from the standpoint of "being alone" and relying on fearful, arrogant, "self-will run riot." The results are not pretty. Ask any of "these little ones," new believers who plunged headfirst into ministry, and I'll bet you will hear some stories of painful falls. Ask any recovering alcoholic after years of sobriety who went through the same prideful, destructive situation and relapsed because they forgot their dependence on God.

"Thine is the kingdom and the power, and the glory forever and ever" - This is an affirmation to remind our subconscious of the truth.

Let's move on to the next area of teaching on love.

"Love your enemy." Sounds like a lofty, altruistic ideal that some may wish to aspire towards intellectually, but it is not something to be taken seriously, right? Wrong. It's an all-important concept of divine love, one that we (believers) are called to grasp and literally implement, along with loving strangers and loving Christ.

"Be morally friendly (*agapo*, love) to those who are in hostile or hateful opposition to you or something you stand for (*phielo*, enemy)." This is certainly one of the most important concepts in all of Jesus's teachings, and one that is ignored by the powers of the world (governments, institutions, policies, television, etc.) I have a serious concern that a majority of us calling ourselves Christian may grossly misunderstand this teaching and its importance. It is the very core of what Christianity is "meant to be," faith in Christ. It is what distinguishes the ideology of "Christ followers" from other religions. I deliberately say Christ followers rather than Christianity here because I am distinguishing between "disciples," those who are committed to studying and following the teachings of Christ Jesus, and the general, institutionalized Christian theology taught, which has managed to accommodate doctrine or theory that goes against the teaching, life, and death of Jesus in which he revealed a trustworthy God of nonviolence and the plan of Salvation for humanity, for the reconciliation of "all things on earth and in heaven." (Ephesians 1:10). Further, I state to you that to truly understand the meaning and significance of Christ's work on the Cross (His love for us), we MUST grasp this concept that He taught. One cannot love Jesus unless they can keep His commands, and we can't share His message if we don't understand it.

Many may mistakenly believe that the New Testament tells us "not to resist evil," that we are just pawns being attacked during spiritual warfare, but are not in the fight, that our role in the Salvation of humanity is to share the gospel with those who want to listen while we wait patiently for Christ to return and set things right.

Big Picture: The New Testament tells us that the embodiment of God's will is executed by God's servants, that "we are to resist evil," just not violently. It says that the "body of Christ" is the human community chartered with manifesting Christ's spirit in the world, that "we" have been "given the keys to heaven;" that "whatever we bind in earth will be bound in heaven;" whatever we "agree about on earth will be done also in heaven." (Matthew 16:19, 18:18-19) We play a significant role in the salvation and reconciliation of humanity on earth, but also for the fallen angels, principalities, and powers in heaven, too.

We are called to preach the truth of the gospel not only to humans, but to angels as well. It is through the Church (believer community, "body of Christ") that "the manifold wisdom of God might be made known to the rulers and authorities in heavenly places." (Ephesians 3:10)

Jesus expects His followers to change things on Earth, not only human things, but heavenly things. The New Testament explains that structural change is not enough; that the heart and soul must also be freed from bondage, forgiven, and united with the Source (God), that standing together through intercessory prayer, believers have access to the presence of God and his power to combat evil powers both materially and spiritually.

"We need to convert people from the spirituality that binds them to a particular material expression of power." (Walter Wink) The reign of God in the New Testament has a new heaven (spirituality) and a new earth (materiality). Both of these, the "inner" and "outer" aspects, must be simultaneously approached for change to occur. The spirit that forms a power must be reached and changed, along with the concrete or material thing (policy, view, government, church, institution, law, etc.)

"For we are contending not against flesh and blood, but against the principalities, against the powers…" What the original writings in Greek say, in effect, is that we contend against "the spirituality of institutions, against ideologies, metaphors, and legitimations that prop them up against greed and coveting that give them life, against the individual egocentricities that powers so easily hook, against idolatry that pits short-term gain against the long-term good of the whole—all of which is manifested only in concrete institutions, systems, structures and persons."

Think of Satan as the "actual power that congeals around collective idolatry, injustice of inhumanity, a power that increases or decreases according to the degree of collective refusal to choose higher values.

At an individual relationship level, Scripture teaches about humility and hypocrisy in looking at your part in conflict: "take the plank out of your own eye before pointing out the splinter in someone else's," and how to diffuse anger with gentleness: "soft words turn away wrath." On a broader level, Jesus teaches that when one responds to the evil actions of others with evil, they have succumbed to joining evil. Both sides are following Satan (the lie).

Jesus was the prototype for humanity to follow, modeling how we should behave. He did not respond to hate with hate or violence with violence. He did not retaliate and fight in defending Himself. He didn't let His disciples engage in physical conflict. He did not kill another human. He had all the power and He did not use it in violence. He didn't lead an army against those who opposed Him. Jesus taught that we must resist evil without becoming evil in the process. Christ refused to compromise on His obedience to the holy righteous ideals of God. He died modeling that to show us the truth, to end scapegoating so that we would love and trust, not hate and fear. "...He humbled Himself and became obedient to the point of death, even death on the cross." (Philippians 2:7-8)

"The violence associated with the God in the Old Testament was centrifuged away, revealing God as a loving parent. The violence of the Powers was exposed, along with their expropriation of God to justify their oppression." The Son came to shed light on the deception under which the world was living. The early Apostles and Disciples understood this teaching, but it is clear that we do not today.

For three centuries following the resurrection of Christ, believers refused to engage in war. Once the church was taken over by the Roman Empire, there was a rationalizing within Christianity of participation in violence and oppression of enemies of "their state." "When the Roman Empire embraced Christianity, one of the results was victory of the empire over the gospel. The 'Church' ceased being the persecuted and became a persecutor," thus following the

Anti-Christ without being aware of it. Early Christian theologian Tertullian said to soldiers who converted to Christianity, "Quit the army or die as martyrs refusing to fight." Later (430 A.D.), it was Augustine, not Jesus, who proposed the theory of "just war." It is hard for me to imagine that it would be God's will for me not to protect my child or the helpless from attack, but at the same time, I am bound to do all that is possible to avoid killing another one of God's children (my spiritual brother).

In order to really understand the teaching of "love thy enemy," we're going to take a look at the historical "Myth of Redemptive Violence" and bring it into our present world. This "myth," the dominant religion in our society today, is not Judaism, Islam, or Christianity. It is the notion that violence saves, of just wars—this is what society believes in.

Satan's Historical Myth: The Enuma Elish (Babylonian creation story) goes like this: Aspu, the father god, and Tiamat, the mother god, give birth to "the gods," but the frolicking of the younger gods makes so much noise that the elder gods resolve to kill them. The younger gods end up killing Aspu, and Tiamat (known as the "dragon of chaos") pledges to get revenge. The young rebel gods turn to their youngest member, Marduk, who kills her. "He catches Tiamat in a net, drives an evil wind down her throat, shoots an arrow that bursts her distended belly, and pierces her heart. He then splits her skull with a club and scatters her blood in out-of-the-way places. He stretches out her cadaver full-length and creates the Cosmos, creating humans from her blood. Here, we see creation as an act of violence: the rebel 'male' god murders and dismembers Tiamat, the feminine dragon of chaos, creating the world from her corpse, thus establishing order. From evil proceeds good, the gods themselves are violent heroes who kill to create order.

The biblical creation story is diametrically opposed to all this.

In Genesis, good is prior to evil; neither evil nor violence is a part of creation. Everything God creates is good. There is a good reality which gets corrupted by fear and selfishness. In the Babylonian myth that violence saves, the hero complex, the concept of a "just holy war," is not a problem to those following the Babylonian religion. In fact, it is what man is called to do by the gods, which we can see reinforced today as "jihad" in the Koran.

They saw the King of Babylon as Marduk's representative on earth, tasked to subdue all enemies who threatened what had been established on behalf of the god. Is this the creation story told by "fallen angels" who according to the Bible, by the way, were the "princes" of the nations in this region? Was this Satan's rendition of things? In the region known as Babylon (Arabia, Syria, Iran, Iraq, Palestine, Israel, etc.) violence has always been a way of life.

This Babylonian myth spread from the Middle East to parts of Africa, the Nordic world, Europe and Asia (Phoenicia, Egypt, Greece, Rome, Germany, Ireland, India, China, etc.) It became the ideology of the status quo, of fallen man, the story of conquest and the victory of order over chaos.

In all of these parts of the world, the creation stories, to paraphrase Professor Walter Wink from his book *The Powers That Be*, "typically involved a male war god residing in the sky (such as Wotan, Zeus, or Indra) who fights with a female god who is depicted as "chaos," a monster, dragon or serpent living in the sea or "abyss." The male victor creates the cosmos from the female "serpent's" corpse and human beings from her blood, who are then slaves to the gods. Creation of the universe requires violent suppression of the feminine, hence what we see in societal subjection of women to men and people to rulers.

In modern times this myth is in the Koran, as I mentioned, but it is also pervasive in Western society, in the spirits of the powers and principalities. "Estimates vary widely, but the average child is reported to log roughly 36,000 hours of television by age eighteen, viewing some 15,000 murders." Video games, movies, and cartoons all portray "good guys killing bad guys," as heroes and as the righteous. In America, individual life seems no longer to be sacred. We are a violent nation, from movies like *Fight Club* and *Friday the 13th* to real world MMA to *Halo, Mortal Combat*, and *Grand Theft Auto* videogames, to the news media hyping phrases like "active shooting." We like violence.

There really isn't such a thing as a "Christian nation, and not only because we don't understand or follow the teachings of Christ, but also because in truth, we are nationalists first and Christians second. We are ready to throw out our values and ideals as soon as they are in conflict with our "nation" (material wealth, comfort, or politics). We arrogantly believe that we are "the righteous people," who have God's support in our aggressions in spite of evidence and teachings to the extreme opposite.

"Many devout Christians simply dismiss Jesus's teaching about nonviolence out of hand as impractical idealism." This is due in part to the common "misunderstanding" of Scripture. The traditional interpretation that most have assumed is that "turn the other cheek" means to submit to abuse, and "go the extra mile" means to extend yourself, and that "let him have your cloak also," means be a doormat, thus making Christians passive victims. It probably makes sense that not many of us are okay with the idea of striving to be a victim. This is absolutely not what the gospel taught. Jesus did not teach non-resistance to evil. He told us to "resist," but without violence.

Let me show you what I mean. You have heard that it was "an eye for an eye and a tooth for a tooth." But I say to you, do not resist an evil doer. But if anyone strikes you on the right cheek, turn the other to him also. If anyone wants to sue you and take away your tunic, let him have your cloak also. And if anyone forces you to go the extra mile, go with him two." (Matthew 5:38-41, also Luke 6:29)

This translation of Greek into English reads: "Do not resist an evildoer," implying nonresistance. What it actually originally said in Greek was "don't react violently to the one who is evil." The Greek word in Matthew 5:39 for "resist" is "*antistenai*," meaning literally to stand (*stenai*) against (*anti*).

Translators may have overlooked that *antistenai* was most often used in the Greek version of the Old Testament as a technical term for warfare, as opposing sides marched towards each other and stood their ground before converging in battle.

Ephesians 6:13 uses *antistenai* exactly this way in counseling us to "resist evil," saying, "Therefore take up the whole armor of God, so that you may be able to withstand (*antistenai*) on that day, and having done everything to stand firm (*stenai*)." Translators working for King James of England did not want people to conclude that they had any recourse against his tyranny. James had "explicitly commissioned a new translation of the Bible because of what he regarded as 'seditious …dangerous, and traitorous' tendencies in the marginal notes of the Geneva Bible."

We can see the same type of liberty being taken by the King James translators when they "added" a qualifier to Matthew 5:23 in support of Augustine's theory that when protecting the interests of your kingdom, there is such a thing as a "just" war, one that Christ supported.

Before the King James Version, the Bible read: "You have heard that it was said to those of old, You shall not murder, and whoever murders will be in danger of judgment. But I say to you that whoever is angry with his brother shall be in danger of the judgment."

The King James Version reads, "whoever is angry at their brother 'without cause,' shall be in danger of their judgment," thus changing Jesus's teaching to imply that it's okay as long as you have a "reason" supporting the notion of just war, or "just killing."

This is an obscene corruption of scripture, because it's the opposite of what Jesus said, and when someone is angry, they always have a cause or reason in mind. So if we kill, it's okay as long as we have a good reason? Most of the modern English Bibles have corrected this error, but it is still found in the NKJV and KJV (New King James Version and King James versions).

"Turn the other cheek:" Jesus was speaking to people who were used to being degraded in Jewish religious communities where the left hand was used only for unclean tasks. It was common for a master or the husband of the house to backhand their non-equal as an insult or form of humiliation. "Turn the other cheek" actually means "refuse to accept this kind of treatment anymore." If I backhand you on your left cheek and you offer your right urging me to strike it, I can't backhand you. I would have to hit you with my open palm. In effect, you would be saying to me, "I'm your equal. If you hit me again, you'll have to do it as such." Now this approach might escalate the anger of the person striking or it might cause them to reflect on their dehumanizing behavior. It might reach their conscience and touch their soul. Either way, the instruction from Jesus is to resist without becoming evil in doing so.

"Go the extra mile:" Same thing here. Roman soldiers were allowed to force any Jew they saw on the road to carry their packs and gear for one mile so they could rest. The instruction from Jesus was if you were treated like a pack mule, rather than fight or just accept it, carry the gear beyond the one-mile limit, causing the soldier to violate their policy, possibly getting them in trouble with a superior, or again perhaps reaching their conscience.

"Give him your cloak also:" Same thing here. If you borrowed money from a person and didn't pay it back on time, that lender could demand extreme interest and could also take you to court, literally suing you for your possessions, including your clothes. Predatory lending was a huge problem back then with the poor being indebted to the rich and often forced into servitude to pay the debt. Here Jesus is saying if this occurs and someone sues for all you have, give him your coat, too. Take off your clothes right in court and embarrass everyone, exposing greed and the evil system supporting it. In this strict religious court, seeing someone naked would cause duress.

What else does the New Testament have to say about loving your enemies? You have heard it said, "You shall love your neighbor and hate your enemy. But I say to you, love your enemies, bless those who curse you, do good to those who spitefully use you and persecute you, that you may be sons of your Father in Heaven; for He makes His sun rise on evil and good, and sends rain on just and the unjust." (Matthew 5:43-46)

"But I say to you who hear: Love you enemies, do good to those who hate you, bless those who curse you, and pray for those who spitefully use you… Give to everyone who asks of you. And from him who takes away your goods, do not ask them back. And just as you want men to do to you, you also do to them likewise. But if you love those who love you, what credit is that to you? For even sinners love those who love them. And if you do good to those who do good to you, what credit is that to you? For even sinners do the same. And if you lend to those from whom you hope to receive back, what credit is that to you? For even sinners lend to sinners to receive much back. But love your enemies, do good, and lend hoping for nothing in return; and your reward will be great, and you will be the sons of the Most High. For He is kind to the unthankful and evil. Therefore be merciful, just as your Father also is merciful." (Luke 6:27-36)

Do these sound like foreign concepts to you, to do something in the name of love, expecting nothing in return? Give, expecting nothing in return? Be kind to the ungrateful and evil? They are foreign concepts, not of this material, spiritually dead world, but of God's (Love's) heavenly world.

Again, Jesus rebukes the notion of capital punishment or just war. "You have heard it said, 'An eye for an eye and a tooth for a tooth.' But I tell you, do not resist an evil person with violence;" "do not react violently against the one who is evil." (Matthew 5:39, scholar's translation) "Do not repay evil for evil." (Romans 12:17). "See that no one renders evil to anyone." (1 Thessalonians 5:15); "not returning evil for evil;" (1 Peter 3:9) "To the contrary, if your enemy is hungry, feed him; if he is thirsty, give him something to drink."

There are many other examples of Jesus rejecting violence, such as Luke 9:51-56, 22:51, and Matthew 26:52.

In today's newspaper, I read an article in which a nine-year-old girl was testifying before Congress about drones. The CIA launched a drone attack in 2012 on her home in Afghanistan. She held up a drawing depicting a drone strike that killed her 67-year-old grandmother, injured her cousin, her 8-year-old sister, and herself (her parents were already dead). She said, "I no longer love blue skies, but prefer gray skies because drones don't fly when it's gray." How many children across the Middle East are traumatized when they look up? How many are afraid of what a blue sky brings? What are humans doing to each other?

Love your neighbor: "You shall love your neighbor as yourself." Jesus is crystal clear about the responsibilities of those who are His followers towards humanity at large.

"This is my commandment, that you love one another as I have loved you,

Love does no harm to a neighbor."

In a dialogue about inheriting eternal life, a lawyer asked Jesus, "And who is my neighbor?" In response, Jesus went into the parable of the good Samaritan, in which a "complete stranger in need was treated like a family member, and the Samaritan looked after him, taking him off the road and putting him up at an inn, paying his way for food and lodging. Jesus said, "You go and do likewise." (Luke 10:25-27)

We are to share what we have with those in need. Believers in Christ understand that all provisions (food, shelter, money, and love) come from God. Therefore, those who "have" are but trusted stewards (administrators) of God's money, food, shelter, blessing, and love. We are entrusted to use these provisions as He would.

We are responsible for behaving in a Christ-like way towards non-believers and believers alike: the homeless, the helpless, the hungry, and the poor.

One of the chief struggles people have with believing in a loving God is that there is so much unkindness and so much suffering in this world, children living on dirt floors without running water, malnourished, afflicted, and lacking access to medical care; unloved people who grow up to be parents who are drug addicts or in prison; random or hate-motivated shootings, ongoing wars, terrorism, and killing across the globe. "Why wouldn't a loving God stop all the bad?" What an amazing, distorted cop-out, "compartmentalizing" and denying our own accountability. We need to reverse that question and ask ourselves why aren't "we" wiping away the unkind suffering? Then we need to accept the answer: it's because the love of God is not in us, or if it is, we repress and deny it. This is all a part of Satan's lie, that we are separated from God. He accuses God and then us.

God gave mankind free will and dominion over the land, air, and sea. This is our domain to take care of and we have all that we need to do it. We simply choose not to because we believe a lie.

We are God's vehicles through which miracles work, through which blessings occur, and through which love is expressed.

In your family, if a child was sick and in his or her room at dinnertime, would someone take them food, or would you simply say to each other, "Why doesn't Good feed him?" Yes, it is "inconvenient" to get up and take a plate of food down the hall, but you would do it. If you loved your neighbor as yourself, you would feed them, too.

The miracle needed to eradicate starvation could be as simple as loving strangers enough to come together and feed them! The uneaten food thrown out from households, restaurants and grocery stores in the U.S. alone would go a long, long way.

When God blesses someone financially, He doesn't make cash appear from thin air, but rather blesses them through a job or with a gift of love from another human in the form of a check. When God expresses love, it is always through His creation, through us, our thoughts and selfless actions.

When you help the needy, you are helping Jesus. When you ignore them, you are turning your back on God. When you love a stranger, you are loving Christ. We must not allow ourselves to get confused about "salvation by faith, not works." What that means is that doing good deeds and attempting to live "self-righteously" while not in Jesus and all that He taught will not lead to salvation. Salvation isn't being a good person, it's overcoming our false notion of God, our existence and separatism. If we believe and follow, then of course we will do good deeds and "bear good fruit," but out of love as expressions of God working through us, not out of our self-will. We can do nothing apart from Christ's indwelling Spirit.

"Do not lay up for yourselves treasures on earth… For where your Treasure is, there your heart will be also." (Matthew 16:19-21)

"…therefore I command you, saying, 'you shall open your hand wide to your brother, to your poor and your needy, in your land.'" (Deuteronomy 15:11)

Note the possessive use of "your" poor, not "the" poor, and the relation as "brother." This is not saying take care of your own, it's saying the poor are yours to take care of, they are your brothers.

Jesus is so clear on this requirement of loving strangers that it is a defining characteristic by which our ultimate salvation is determined. He explains how it is obvious who has faith (who believes, who is a follower) and who does not, who finds their way into heaven and who does not. "For I was hungry and you gave me no food; I was thirsty and you gave me no drink; I was a stranger and you did not welcome me, sick and in prison and you did not visit me…" "Truly I say to you, inasmuch as you did not do it to the least of these, you did not do it for me." (Matthew 25:42-45)

When the Bible details the virtues of the ideal wife, it says, "She extends her hand to the poor, yes she reaches out her hands to the needy." (Proverbs 31:20) When a man who kept the Commandments not to commit adultery or murder, not to steal or bear false witness, and who honored his father and mother, asked Jesus about the inheritance of eternal life, Jesus said to him, "You still lack one thing. Sell all that you have and distribute it to the poor, and you will have treasure in heaven; and come follow me." (Luke 18:18-22)

"But whoever has the world's goods and sees his brother in need, and shuts up his heart from him, how does the love of God abide in him? (John 3:12)

Fear (lack of faith and trust in God) keeps the average one of us from living this way. "We barely have enough for ourselves. How can we give to others?" we think.

I know a couple who when they first met went on a date dirt-bike riding together. Later, when they were married, the wife felt compelled to sell their motorcycles and use the proceeds to bring love to the homeless. They prayed together and the husband agreed. They went on to have several children, and the husband/father, an electrician, commuted two and a half hours each day to support them. This didn't stop them from giving away one of their two cars for the needy when they had a house full of toddlers. This family does not live in luxury, and I do not believe they are financially "well off," but they didn't wait until they had excess to share what they had. They believed that God wants them to care for their neighbors and that He will always provide all that they need. This is how God blesses people. We are often the miracle God brings into someone's life. Another time they raised money and anonymously bought a car for a fellow believer, leaving a note that God wanted to bless him. I've done this kind of thing, too: paying the mortgage for someone who was at risk of losing their home to foreclosure when I didn't have enough money to pay my bills that month; or taking in a stranger who needed a place to live and helping them get their life on track. That same family whose mortgage I contributed to had a young stranger living with them for a year while he went to school. None of us, as a result of sharing, have ever gone without food or shelter.

In fact, if you really have faith, if you really believe in love, you can care for your neighbors even when you possess nothing materially to share. When I was a young boy, my mother and stepfather were friends with a couple, Reggie and Lee. Reggie was a most extraordinary man in the way that he lived. His home was open to all and he believed that all humans were his loving fellows. He would greet people as newfound family members, expressing love and kindness. If Reggie didn't have what his neighbor needed, he would take that person to another stranger's house, knock on the door and ask. Miraculously, they would get invited in for food and a visit, making new "family" connections, and the following Christmas you would see both sets of those new friends at Reggie and Lee's Christmas party (or open house, as they called it). As a kid, I loved and trusted him, but thought his behavior was weird. Today, looking back, I was blessed to witness a family living not within the normal standards of "this world," but living as Christ taught. As Paul said, "I speak not as a command, but to prove by the earnest of others that your love is also genuine. For you know that the grace of our Lord Jesus Christ, that though He was rich, yet for your sake He became poor, so that you by His poverty might become rich." (2 Corinthians 8:8-9)

"But when you give a feast, invite the poor, the maimed, the lame, the blind (parolees, recovering addicts, the homeless). And you will be blessed because they cannot repay you..." (Luke 14:13)

Love among believers (true Christians): There is a special bond within a community of fellow believers, otherwise known as the "body of Christ," a real sense of connectedness and unity, something that once experienced, will change you.

I was not raised a Christian. In fact, I was more than forty years old when I realized that I believed in and loved the Spirit of Jesus, but from that moment on, I've felt passionately called to be involved in discipleship and ministry. I was blessed to be given the opportunity to jump right in and become deeply committed at the first church I regularly attended, and owe a special thanks to the head Pastor of that church, who became a dear friend. I had the privilege of being baptized in front of a genuine group of people, and then serving as the leader of their men's ministry and recovery ministry, as well as participating in the church's theology and pastor training.

I've been fortunate to learn and experience so much in a short time, being involved in all kinds of church projects and events from building drama sets for productions and summer camps, to working on remodeling the church building or doing community outreach events, to running sound for worship music, or creating multimedia presentations for services, and helping out with youth ministry or facilitating small Bible study groups.

Through this involvement with the church and fellow believers, I have experienced a kind of kinship different from anything I've known before, where people I'd just met were the people I was incorporating into my day-to-day life in dinners, lunches, birthdays, holidays—helping each other with household projects and in church ministry. I've never felt more peaceful and connected to a group of people than when working hand-in-hand beside fellow believers who share a common love for Christ and each other.

To have a "real" community of people to do life with is amazingly special, and quite foreign. As an example, I remember one time when my wife, step-children and I moved to a new home 45 minutes away from our old one to be nearer to our church, and twenty-four people from the church showed up to help, making several trips back and forth. By the end of the day, our new home was literally set up. The washer and dryer were connected, the dishes were unpacked and put away, the five beds put together and made, and most of our pictures and paintings were mounted on the walls. Those were true friends expressing God's love, and you could feel it. It was amazing.

The Bible instructs believers to love each other just this way, to support one another, share what you have, show up in times of need, to build each other up spiritually, to serve side-by-side in the common cause, and to hold each other accountable.

"He who was in the form of God, did not count equality with God a thing to be grasped, but emptied Himself by taking the form of a servant, being born in the likeness of men. And being found in human form, He humbled Himself by becoming obedient to the point of death, even death on a cross." (Philippians 2:1-8)

As we are to do: "Let love be without hypocrisy. Abhor what is evil. Cling to what is good. Be kindly affectionate to one another, not lagging in diligence, fervent in spirit, serving the Lord; rejoicing in hope, patient in tribulation, continuing steadfastly in prayer, distributing to the needs of the saints (believers), given to hospitality." (Romans 12:9)

As you and I are called to do: "He who loves his brother abides in the light, and there is not cause for stumbling in him." (Galatians 3:28)

There is no cause for us to sin, no reason for us to struggle. **If we truly love** our fellows.

When Christ, through His work on the cross, exposed our false notion of God, removing our hostility and changing our relationship with God to one of trust, we were then given the "ministry of reconciliation," entrusted as God's ambassadors to tell all others that they, too, can trust God and be restored to their true purpose in relationship with Him.

"…as though God were pleading through us…" (2 Corinthians 5:14-21)

God's plan involves uniting "all things," reconciling evil to good, "making known to us the mystery of His will, according to His purpose, which He set forth in Christ as a plan to unite all things in Him, things in heaven and things on earth." (Ephesians 1:10)

You and I, if we believe in Jesus, in what He said, are tasked with playing an important role in this plan. Together, believers are to become vessels for God's grace and love to stream through. It is through you and me that God's wisdom (His ways and His plan) is made known, not just to creatures on earth, but to angels in heaven too. They learn by seeing God's grace working through us.

"The manifold wisdom of God is made known by the church (by believers, the body of Christ) to the principalities and powers in heavenly places according to the eternal purpose realized in Jesus." (Ephesians 3:9-10)

The battle to be waged in heaven and on earth involves us; we are Christ's soldiers, if you will. We are not battling what is seen, but rather the demonic spirits of those fallen angels and their offspring, evil spirits that attach themselves to people (sometimes without their knowledge) and influence our systems, governments, and institutions.

We are called to model real love, to cast out demons, to put light on the darkness, to preach the gospel of Jesus, and to pray expectantly for their reconciliation, thanking God in advance of heaven, whatever we collectively agree to on earth will occur, both on earth and in heaven. (READ Matthew 16:19 and 18:18.)

This is why unity among believers is critical. We have an important job to do and we cannot afford to take it lightly. We are called to bring change through the Spirit of Christ, to share the message of reconciliation and salvation, to bind God's will on earth, to reach souls, powers, and principalities that are fallen or lost, calling for their change through the intercession of our prayer. We **CANNOT** accomplish God's will as separate-thinking individuals, but **WE CAN** as His healthy, united body:

"...being like-minded," (Ephesians 2:21) "...having the same love," (John 17:21) "being of one accord," ("a togetherness of soul") (1 Corinthians 12:13) "...we know that we have passed from death to life, **BECAUSE** we love the brethren. He who does not love his brother abides in death. Whoever hates his brother is a murderer, and you know that no (ends here, p. 178)

God's love for you and me: Let me paint a picture of humanity as Jesus did for His ministry. We [mankind] as a whole had a distorted notion of God, all religious and non-religious people alike. Our notion of God was that He was punitive and untrustworthy. We twisted His words to mean what we wanted, justifying our ungodly behavior, projecting attitudes of violence, racism, sexism, and favoritism onto God, when He has none of those. We were "missing the mark," (sinning) across the board, failing to meet our designed purpose of expressing God's creative intelligence, beauty, and love; failing to administer harmony in the environment over which He gave us dominion.

Now imagine what it must be like for God, being the Spirit of

Love, and watching each individual person as an extension of His Spirit, as His "children," abusing one another, sometimes in His name.

Imagine seeing and feeling all of the evil, destructive behavior of your children as they selfishly lie, cheat, and steal from each other, as they seek to dominate, oppress, and enslave each other.

Imagine hearing your daughters cry as their husbands and children are brutally murdered, or feeling your son's heartache and bewilderment as his wife betrays him with another man, or as he watches his family starve to death.

Imaging your children stepping over each other to get what they want in greedy lust, ignoring their siblings who are in dire need.

Now imagine that you know the reason why they do these things is not because they are inherently evil, but because they were told a lie and believe it. The lie is that you don't love them, that you won't provide for them, that you won't protect them, that you don't have their best interests at heart, that you have abandoned them—that maybe you don't even really exist. Either way, they believe they are alone to fend for themselves in this violent, dangerous world. And you know that this is compounded by the perpetrator of the lie, as he accuses your children of being inherently bad and worthless, as he hacks away at their character, weakening their resolve.

So you manifest a part of yourself into the world in the flesh to expose the deception we live under and all of our distorted notions, to teach us about Love, to model the true relationship we should have with you as your spiritual sons and daughters.

Because as Jesus, you are paving the way for a new humanity to follow, you have been committed to experiencing life as a man, to show us that **we** can believe to the point of God's power working through us, to show us that we can conform to God's will and be the expression of God's Love.

As Jesus on earth, while you are wholly God, you were born as a human with the limitations of man, so your access to God's power comes to you by overcoming those limitations, through absolute belief in the power, grace, and love of the Father, just as you say it should for God's other sons and daughters, through absolute belief, absolute faith, and absolute obedience to the will of our Father in heaven.

As a man, He did not have peace of mind. Jesus was often frustrated, sad, and sometimes depressed. He was lonely, and struggled with fear and anxiety. What He did as a man was scary. At every decision point, He committed Himself to doing the "right thing," when doing the wrong thing would likely get Him out of trouble, out of pain and physical death.

He overcame fear and temptation with belief and faith. He prayed constantly for emotional strength and guidance.

So imagine what this was like, imagine how it must have felt. When someone hits you, it hurts. You feel heartache when betrayed by a friend. You're watching humanity mistreating each other and it breaks your heart because you love them all. You feel frustration, sorrow, and despair as it becomes clearer to you that we just "won't get it," we won't collectively wake up, and your Father reveals to you His plan that ultimately, you must let us kill you in order to prove to us that you are loving and trustworthy, that you are who you say you are, that the notion of God you teach is the Truth, and that how we see things (through Satan's deception) is false.

As a man you don't want to leave your mother, brothers, students, Mary, and dear friends. You are afraid of the unknown, of the physical anguish you will have to endure, of being nailed to a cross with your body weight tearing your muscles and bones apart as you slowly bleed to death.

And you have great sorrow knowing the broken hearts of those who love you as they stand and watch you die. As a man you wish there were another way, but you will go forward because you love humanity and you love your Father.

> "Now My soul is troubled, and what shall I say? Father, save Me from this hour? But for this purpose I come for this hour. Father, glorify Your name. Then a voice came from heaven saying, 'I have glorified it and will glorify it again.' The crowd that stood there and heard it said that it was thundered... Jesus answered, 'This voice has come for your sake, not mine... now the ruler of this world (fear of death, Satan) will be cast out. And I, when I am lifted up from earth, will draw all people to Myself." (John 12:27-30)

Imagine how deep and strong your love would have to be to be willing to die this way to prove to those you love that you are speaking Truth. It's a kind of courageous, selfless, and loyal love that is stronger than anything, even death. Jesus said, "If anyone loves Me, he will obey (listen to, believe, and heed) My teaching. My Father will love him, and we will make our home with Him. He who does not love Me will not obey My teaching." (John 14:23)

Remember, love is not just personal sentiment as we many times mistakenly think. Love is selfless action, the expression of God's ideas.

Jesus made it simple: "If you don't follow My teaching, you don't love Me." And we cannot obey Him if we don't believe Him and all that He said. "For it is not the hearers of the law who are righteous, but the doers of the law (the law being "to love")." (Romans 2:13).

At any given moment, we are either driven by Love or fear, by one or the other, by the Truth or "the lie."

Our journey towards spiritual maturity, of increasing faith, working out our salvation, can be directly measured by the fullness with which we express love (obey God)—the degree to which we are true expressions of God. This is what "faith not works" is talking about.

Shortly before His murder, Jesus expresses His love for "all" of us as He prays for Himself, His disciples, and all believers who come to the Truth later.

JESUS PRAYS FOR HIS DISCIPLES

6 "I have manifested Your name to the men whom You have given Me
out of the world. They were Yours, You gave them to Me, and they
have kept Your word. 7 Now they have known that all things which
You have given Me are from You. 8 For I have given to them the words
which You have given Me; and they have received *them,* and have
known surely that I came forth from You; and they have believed
that You sent Me.

9 "I pray for them. I do not pray for the world but for those whom
You have given Me, for they are Yours. 10 And all Mine are Yours, and
Yours are Mine, and I am glorified in them. 11 Now I am no longer in
the world, but these are in the world, and I come to You. Holy Father,
keep through Your name those whom You have given Me,[b] that they
may be one as We *are.* 12 While I was with them in the world,[c] I kept
them in Your name. Those whom You gave Me I have kept;[d] and
none of them is lost except the son of perdition, that the scripture
might be fulfilled. 13 But now I come to You, and these things I speak
in the world, that they may have My joy fulfilled in themselves. 14 I
have given them Your word; and the world has hated them because
they are not of the world, just as I am not of the world. 15 I do not pray
that You should take them out of the world, but that You should keep

them from the evil one. 16 They are not of the world, just as I am not
of the world. 17 Sanctify them by Your truth. Your word is truth. 18 As
You sent Me into the world, I also have sent them into the world. 19
And for their sakes I sanctify Myself, that they also may be sanctified
by the truth.

JESUS PRAYS FOR ALL BELIEVERS

20 "I do not pray for these alone, but also for those who will[e] believe in
Me through their word; 21 that they all may be one, as You, Father, *are*
in Me, and I in You; that they also may be one in Us, that the world may
believe that You sent Me. 22 And the glory which You gave Me I have
given them, that they may be one just as We are one: 23 I in them, and
You in Me; that they may be made perfect in one, and that the world may
know that You have sent Me, and have loved them as You have loved Me.

24 "Father, I desire that they also whom You gave Me may be
with Me where I am, that they may behold My glory which You have
given Me; for You loved Me before the foundation of the world. 25 O
righteous Father! The world has not known You, but I have known
You; and they have known that You sent Me. 26 And I have declared
to them Your name, and will declare *it,* that the love with which You
loved Me may be in them, and I in them."

The other part of you, the Father, is willing to have His beloved Son go through all of this because he loves all of us and longs to spend eternity with us. He loves us too much not to save us from being separated from Him forever.

His plan is for love to change the world: "Yes, I have loved you (God says to you and me) with an everlasting love; Therefore, with loving kindness (a covenant of loyalty) I have drawn you. Again I will build you, and you shall be rebuilt (freed from bondage and re-established in His love.)" (Jeremiah 31:3)

Loving God: So, what does it really mean to love God? The simplest statement is that loving God means obeying Him, which entails genuinely loving each other.

Within our church communities there is a tendency to conform to popular opinion. We've accepted society's values, trends, and traditions, mistakenly thinking that following those rules makes us righteous people. If we love Jesus, we have a mandate to follow the path He walked as a non-conformist who confronted injustice always! To love God is to emulate Jesus. We have to stand against hatred and racism. We must step out of comfort, and not define success by worldly standards. To love Jesus well we must fight for all people, not against them. We can't allow our institutions to stray off course. They can't protect themselves and need our help to preserve decency.

If you love Jesus for real, you'll be courageous and stand against everything in opposition to the teachings of Christ. The church of Christ Jesus must reclaim the power and authority He entrusted us with, which can only happen by conforming to the demands of His teaching.

9

HUMAN BEINGS – YOU AND I

OUR IDENTITY

Who are you? What are you? Have you ever really taken a moment to wonder about us? Humans are truly amazing and magnificent beings. Think about us. The human body is astonishing, with skin that shields, muscles and bones as the framing, the complex machinery of our nervous system, nerves, arteries, veins, ligaments, tendons, vertebrae, discs, joints, cartilage, fibers, a heart that pumps blood, lungs that breathe oxygen, fingers, hands, arms and legs that allow us to move physically with great precision. We have eyes that see beauty, a mouth with a unique voice to talk and sing, and ears that hear, and we're mostly water.

What about DNA, the written instructions and motor contained inside us, that literally creates, repairs, and maintains life. How does that happen? The information contained in a single DNA strand, if strung out, would be more than five feet in length, and yet all of the cells in our body put together could be compressed to the size of a golf ball. Yet from that DNA, we can tell who our great grandfather was and where he came from. We are only 3% to 5% genetically unique. The other 95% to 97% is the same among all living things.

What about all the little miracles we perform and take for granted, like throwing a basketball into a hoop 10 feet in the air from 30 feet away with absolute precision, sometimes while running? Or that if after you release the ball, if you "doubt" that it will go in, it won't? How about holding your breath and swimming underwater, riding horses, and having relationships with dogs and cats? What about dancing to music, or playing an instrument? How about the big miracle of partnering to create a new human?

What about our mind? We have thoughts we're consciously aware of, do background processing of information 24 hours a day, and receive correct information from this thing called intuition. We process 10 trillion thought transactions a second from the 3-5% of our brain that we have access to.

Is it a coincidence that the mind and the cosmos are both approximately 95% unsearchable and DNA in all living things is also about 95% the same, and that our make-up is about 95% water? If you looked through a telescope at a galaxy and then at a picture of the brain's electric charges, you might not be able to tell the difference.

What little I've learned about any of this from a scientific standpoint leaves me in awe! As it turns out, science shows that physically we are not even "ourselves," but are actually trillions of vibrating, osculating bundles of dynamic energy. Each of the properties that make particles have "their own will" and interact with each other on our behalf. This energy that makes us up cannot be destroyed. It is eternal.

Despite any of the destructive things we do, we are truly a beautiful and masterful piece of work; amazing technology. The Bible says that we are made to be the reflection of God's Spirit on the physical plane. We are like reflections of light off water.

Have you noticed that as machinery or technology our most basic function is to reflect thoughts, ideas, and beliefs? Regardless of who we are, where we come from or what we believe in, we will always be reflections or expressions of what we believe, perhaps distorted ones, but reflections, nonetheless.

In the movie *The Matrix*, people live in a very oppressive material world, void of emotion and love, where exercising free will is punishable by death. A group of them discover that their reality is a deception, a lie used to keep them in bondage. They surmise that all they have to do is believe in this "truth, shedding all fear," and then their thoughts will lead to victory and freedom to live in their real world as their authentic selves. To enter into battle with evil they plug into a supercomputer that simulates physical scenarios, a virtual reality. It's extremely dangerous, because what they believe to be true is their reality. If the hero believes that he's been shot, he will then literally, physically die. This level of mind control only works if he believes 100%, with no doubts. Like most good vs. evil stories, the hero comes through against all odds, and at the last minute. He does so presumably because he was the 'chosen one' whom God selected to defeat evil because he 'would believe.' This all sounds pretty good, but here's the gotcha. It does not work because they are still under the spell of deception. The part about thoughts creating reality, that's true. The requirement to believe 100% with no doubts, that's true; and even being chosen for the task because "he would believe," that works. The problem is that they will never win as long as they use evil [violent force] to fight evil. The saga continues in numerous sequels, with no one living in harmony, love or peace. They are still in bondage, but now to a life of violence and war. The deception is so cunning, so brilliant really, that it has them believing that the struggle between oppression and freedom, between good and evil can be won through violent force. Using evil to fight evil simply ensures that all is corrupt and evil continues. Evil protects itself with this subversive lie.

This is the paradox Jesus was teaching about.

Truth: Freedom from oppression will not come through violent force (evil). The oppressor cannot be forced to change (repeat and receive redemption) from the outside; it must come from within. The oppressor must come to believe in the Truth and love, in order for good and evil to be reconciled, thus expressing harmony or health, prosperity, and happiness (the holy ideas of God).

This is Love's (God's) heart's desire (will, or *thelema* in Greek) for us, the blueprint (purpose, *prothesis* in Greek) for our lives.

So some of our most fundamental beliefs, things we inherently take for granted, things we grow up accepting as truth, are in fact lies. These untruths have been perpetuated for thousands of years across most civilizations and under many religions (including Christianity). They go unchecked as long as they are invisible to us. It's a deception that accounts for a social ethic of justified domination, which involves violence and humiliation, allows for starvation and the eradication of life, war, the subjection/objectification of women, for toxic corporations, corrupt politics, and the destruction of our environment. It is the perversion of all of that which is just. It is specifically what Jesus was talking about in addressing darkness, evil, wickedness, and Satan.

Today we get socialized as we grow up through systems of thought, which are under the same "spell" of deception. So it's embedded in what's portrayed on television, in movies, video games, at school, and through our parents, friends, and society. Before we are old enough to choose what we believe in, we are indoctrinated into the "world," the one Jesus says Satan rules through lies. A world where people and nations are driven by and worship power, money, sex, and the accumulation of material possessions.

In this world people desire to be above others, on top, elite. We want to be special and to matter, but their perceived importance is based on what they have, and not who they are.

The battle of good and evil then, is really the spiritual one of thought. Do I believe that God is trustworthy or not? Because if He is, I don't need to be separate, I don't need to fuel the deception of being a separate self (Ego edging God out).

From my personal perspective, "ego" was initiated at the point of "The Lie" (Original Sin). When the Bible says we are born to a sinful nature, it is talking about the ego. Our true nature, our real self, is that of God. You can decrease the ego, perhaps even squash it, and increase the Christ in you (indwelling spirit), but only by believing that God is trustworthy.

This is Salvation, it's what we call believing in Christ—not just that Jesus existed, but that everything He said and did was the truth.

Here's why. We are created to love and be loved (the ultimate expression of God), mini instances of God's spirit, our souls long to fulfill this purpose, anything less is untrue.

Think about it. All of our fears can be traced back to love, and all of our destructive, sinful thoughts, behaviors, and actions can be traced back to fear. We are only really afraid that we won't find love, or that we'll lose it; all of our fears roll up into that. It's the motivator behind being martial, why we try to dominate others, why we abuse people or take abuse (co-dependency), why we lie, rob, cheat, and kill. We want to be accepted, we want to matter, we want someone to care if we love them, we want to be loved.

Our ultimate fear is death. Why? Because we think that love will end, that we will lose the ability to express love (our soul's divine purpose).

The lie told so many years ago still has us thwarting love, for love's sake.

"Truth is always strange, stranger than fiction." — Lord Byron

Truth: There is a realm outside of the one we are conscious of, one that is not material, but invisible, an ethereal realm where spirits, advocate and adversaries exist. Most of the time, we only catch glimpses of it.

Typically, we wish to dismiss these as dramatic, superstitious notions, but that is not the case. We can choose not to accept it, but being unaware does not mean it's not there, just simply that we are too uncomfortable, weirded out, or afraid of the idea. Most of us, however, would admit that spiritual or unexplained things do occur.

Lots of people have had premonitions through dreams or visions that have come true, and there have been many unexplainable physical healings.

Truthfully, most of us have had our own experiences or encounters with this realm, but either brush them off as "coincidences," don't like thinking about them, or are sure others would think us weird if we tried to talk about them. This could include things like thinking or talking about someone you're not expecting to hear from only moments before they call ("I was just talking about you, how weird,") or déjà vu, where you know something happened before, or randomly having a thought pop into your head like, "I know what he or she is thinking," or your intuition of impending danger; or perhaps, something more dramatic like feeling the presence of a dead loved one weeks after they die, or seeing something not human.

Our rational mind wants to rule this stuff out, but that is actually a lie. This deception is what the Bible calls spiritual warfare and unbelief, and what psychology calls neurosis.

At the risk of your judging me, to make a point, I'll share a real experience and encounter of a guy I know. During a rough period in his marriage, he was separated from his wife, and in turn, estranged from his four stepchildren for a month. When he came home, everything was out of sorts. What used to be an ordered house was chaotic, everyone's behavior was out of control, everything was out of place and out of balance. He was greeted with tears and a group hug from his four stepchildren, while his wife watched. Early that evening they all (wife and kids) fell asleep cuddled in his arms, watching television. There was a total sense of calm after the storm, of peace and balance being restored. This was something he had been praying for constantly. For weeks he had been asking God to honor the promise to reconcile his marriage and restore his family, and it really appeared that God was orchestrating just that. His wife was still standoffish, so he slept on the couch that night. He couldn't seem to get to sleep and started tossing and turning. All of a sudden it got really cold and fear popped into his mind. He thought, "Whoa," and had the strong feeling of physical danger around him. He got goosebumps and the hair on the back of his neck was tingling. The air got dense and heavy. It was hard to breathe. These are the thoughts that went through his mind:

"'It' wants to stop us from being a family, we're trying to follow God, and "it" wants to tear us apart… It does not want us united as a couple in ministry and raising children who know God. It sees this marriage and family as a threat." He closed his eyes and audibly in his head he said, "I belong to Christ, this family is of God, you can't have us. I rebuke you in the name of Jesus." The room got super cold and he opened his eyes to a hissing sound, and a black, smoky essence slithering over his body about 20 inches above him. He felt as if it was trying to engulf him, and could sense its hatred. He rebuked it again with authority, commanding it to leave. It hissed with great irritation and suddenly was sucked away into the air like a genie vapor back into a bottle. He thought, that was terrifying, and right at that moment the bedroom door opened and his wife came into the living room. It was 3am. She saw that he was awake and asked if he was okay. She said, "I've been awake for a while. Something woke me up and I've been in there praying for you. It felt like there was an oppressive spirit attacking you. He simply said, "Yeah, it was," and they didn't discuss it again. If she had not come out and said what she did, he would have most likely rationalized that he had just had his first panic attack, and wow! Is that what they're like? He would have told himself that logically he was really stressed about trying to hold his family together, but he would have known that there was a lot more to it, not just because of the visual, but because of the room temperature and the feeling of physical danger.

The truth is that whether we call them advocates and adversary spirits, angels and demons, Godly and ungodly ideas, or the more rational sounding, positive and negative thoughts, all are correct labels that identify the truth about spiritual existence and the power of thought.

One thing to note is that we as individuals have the ability to create what the Bible calls abomination, condemnation, and desolation by allowing our minds to think negative thoughts. At the same time, we do not create all the evil that exists: there are other evil-producing entities out there. However, they have no influence over us unless we give it to them.

When he thinks back to that night on the couch, he knows that he was allowing himself to dwell on doubt long enough to have doubts about God being able to pull it off, or doubts that He (God) was really orchestrating reconciliation in the first place. It was his unbelief that gave the demon permission to mess with him.

"...be strong in the Lord and in the power of His might. Put on your whole armor of God, that you may be able to stand against the wiles of the devil. For we do not wrestle against flesh and blood but against principalities, against powers, against rulers of darkness... against spiritual hosts (thoughts) of wickedness (spells of deception, doubt, fear, self-condemnation, and unbelief in Christ's teachings) in the heavenly places (in your mind, your higher consciousness)."

My whole marriage went that way, a series of trials and tests of faith, right at the heart of our deepest fears (abandonment, fidelity, and loyalty), and when I had faith about God's hand in my marriage, the most impossible fell into place. But there was a constant barrage of tests and attacks, and my faith gave way to pride, ego, and fear more frequently than I'd like to admit. I unknowingly conducted this experiment many times over six years, and looking back, it seems like scientific proof of faith and fear.

Our three-dimensional view of reality is more comfortable because we tell ourselves it's fixed, it's rational. Could it be that what we think and what we believe manifests in the physical realm?

The power of positive thinking does wonders. Prayer and love heals sickness, while negative thinking brings on disease, cancer, and other health problems. This is so widely accepted that the medical profession tries to incorporate positive, peaceful, spiritual thought into treatment for serious illness.

I know of several cases, personally, where people diagnosed with critical conditions had their illness vanish without medical explanation. In each of these cases, lots of people were praying for their healing. One woman had a brain tumor that miraculously vanished the night before her brain surgery. When the surgeon did the final scan in preparation for surgery, he was stunned: it made absolutely no medical sense at all. It was as if there had never been a tumor. There were hundreds of people petitioning God for her healing that morning.

Then there was a man with heart disease and a woman with kidney failure, both similar stories My stepson was born prematurely, at 1-1/2 pounds. He could fit in the palm of my hand. The doctors suggested that if he lived, he would have brain damage and motor function problems. For months his mom's church prayed for him, I mean as a group, really prayed week after week. Miraculously he pulled through every touch-and-go life-threatening moment, without medical explanation. According to rational thought he shouldn't be the gregarious, smart, funny, happy, healthy, and vibrant kid he is today. This kid has a zeal for life. He wakes up with a sparkle in his eyes and a huge smile on his face. Today, he's playing on sports teams like any other active kid.

When I was twenty, my aunt was diagnosed with breast cancer. It was really sad. She had two young daughters and a husband. She had both breasts and all of her lymph nodes surgically removed, and did chemo and radiation treatment, but it did not work. She was told that it was fatal, and that she had six months to live. I spent an afternoon alone with her to say our goodbyes.

We laughed, cried, and tenderly talked about spiritual things. She spent a lot of time each day out in nature praying and meditating, focusing on positive thought, beauty, and harmony. She seemed to find inner peace and believed that the cancer would leave before she died. That was almost thirty years ago, and right now she's on vacation in Italy. She retired from a long career as a grade-school teacher. She had a miraculous remission. The cancer had no power over her, so it went away. There are way too many examples like these around the world to consider the possibility that they are random coincidences, and cellular biology, as we've noted, tells us they're not.

How about this: the real you, the spiritual being, your soul as an individualization of the Divine Spirit (God) has a direct link through your intuitive mind (ethereal self) to God.

When we "believe" and conceptualize God's ideas into our conscious minds, they are realized (manifested into the physical). You can effect real changes in the world by renewing your mind. Jesus instructs, "You will say to the mountain, 'move from here to there,' and it will move; nothing will be impossible for you." (Matthew 17:20).

WHAT SCIENCE SAYS

If we look at ourselves today from modern science's perspective (cellular biology and epigenetic research), each of us is a multi-cellular community (~50 trillion cells) influenced by environmental signals known as invisible matter-shaping energy fields (or spirits).

Genes don't control biology, and we **literally** do not end when the physical body dies.

As it turns out, the protein "switches" that control life are primarily turned on and off by signals from the environment… the Universe (God). The cell engages in behavior when its brain, the membrane, responds to environmental signals. Every functional protein in our body is made as a complementary "image" of an environmental signal. If a protein did not have a complementary signal to couple with, it would not function. Every protein in our body is a physical/electromagnetic complement to something in the environment. Because we are machines made out of protein, by definition we are made in the image of the environment, that environment being the Divine Universe/God.

While we are not "ourselves" one member but many (~50 trillion), each of us has a unique biological identity. Identity receptors, called self-receptors (or HLA), are related to the functions of the immune system. Each cell's unique identity receptors are located on the membrane's outer surface, where they act as "antennae," downloading complementary environmental signals. They read a signal of "self," which does not exist within the cell, but comes from the external environment.

The human body is like a TV set. We are the image on the screen, but our image didn't come from inside the TV: it came from the broadcast that is received via the antenna.

Our **real self (soul)** exists in the environment, whether our physical body is here or not.

Each of us is a spirit/ether-based identity that permeates or blends into a molecular suit of vibrating, oscillating cells, cells that are made up of particles, which are made up of properties, which we now know to have dynamic will. These properties get together and decide their course of action in supporting the community (you). There are receptor proteins which are antennae that read vibrational energy fields (spirit, chi, quantum fields), which alter the protein's charge, causing it to change shape. Then there are effector proteins, or behavior-controlling proteins.

Biological behavior can be controlled by invisible forces, including thought. Today's science shows that biology adapts to our beliefs and filters. When we change the way we perceive the world, that is, when we change our beliefs, we literally change our neurochemical composition.

As wild as it sounds, from a scientific perspective, our body is a molecular suit, so to speak, that forms in and around our essence (or spirit). The membrane that acts as the glue between all the vibrating moving properties and particles, literally holding us together, is called lamin. When you look at lamin under a microscope here's what you see:

An epitaph Ben Franklin wrote about himself:

Ben Franklin Boston 1706 devout Calvinist
The body of B. Franklin - Freemason
Printer
Like the cover of an old book,
Its contents torn out
And

Stripped of its lettering and gilding,
Lies here
Food for worms,
But the work shall not be wholly lost,
For it will, as he believed,
Appear once more,
In a new and more perfect edition
Revised and corrected
By the author.

Now imagine that "you," the ethereal, spiritual self, inhabit a physical body that is like a highly sophisticated and technologically advanced suit or costume. Imagine that you penetrate and permeate the molecules and blend into the tissue, structures, and physical form, or rather that it all formed in and around you. Seriously, take a minute right now, maybe close your eyes and try to picture yourself as a spiritual being fully integrated with the composite, vibrating molecular suit. If you give it an honest try, I wonder if you can mentally see the real you. Do you look the same but more transparent, maybe a bit taller? Are you a certain color? I'll bet those of you who spend a few minutes trying to visualize this right before you fall asleep will be intrigued by what happens. Try it!

We're not going to discuss the miraculousness of our "garment" or suit, because there are volumes of books on the anatomy and chemistry of the human body. I do want to talk about the mind, though. When the Bible speaks of the "heart," it's actually talking about the mind, and not suggesting that the blood-pumping organ thinks or feels. The heart was a common euphemism for the mind in the ancient Middle East. Now when we come to the mind and think of ourselves existing without a physical body, we might get stuck because we believe thought and emotion originate chemically from the physical brain tissue.

Take everything you have read so far about physics, atoms, particles, and about ourselves as energy (ethereal-spiritual beings) and apply this train of thought. Imagine that your spirit (pneuma, etheric body), which houses your soul (psyche or *nephesh* in Hebrew), integrates with the physical body as suggested. The soul (intellect, feelings, personality, self) permeates the "Inner Brain," the part of our brain that is hidden from view. It lies in the structures that are gatekeepers between the cerebral hemispheres (left and right lobes or sections). The brain molecules pervade our soul. These "Inner Brain" structures determine our emotional state, perceptions, and responses. This idea is total conjecture on my part but fits with a scientific view. I'm imagining that it's these specific structures that blend or permeate our "etheric mind." These brain structures are the "hypothalamus," the "thalamus," and the "hippocampus." The hypothalamus is the size of a pearl, and directs a multitude of important functions. It wakes you up, gets adrenaline flowing when needed, and it's the emotional center, controlling the molecules that make you feel exhilarated, angry, unhappy, etc. The thalamus then, is the major clearinghouse of information going to and from the spinal cord and the cerebrum. And the hippocampus is an arching tract of nerve cells from the hypothalamus to the thalamus, a tiny hub that acts as a memory indexer, sending memories out to the appropriate part of the hemisphere for long-term storage and retrieval when necessary.

Personally, long before I could read or anyone talked to me about God or spiritual stuff, I had an absolute knowledge (intuition) that my existence went beyond the physical, but it's not something I tried to articulate.

I guess from my perspective all this stuff makes sense, and converges to support what the Bible teaches us. It makes a lot more sense than just imagining that we are neurotic animals who can't stop obsessing about what and who we are, and by some random organic chance just happen to be the products of insanely sophisticated biochemical technology.

Just today, as I was finishing up this section of the chapter, two physicists, Takaaki Kajian and Arthur McDonald, were awarded the Nobel Prize for discovering that "neutrinos" (3 types of tiny subatomic particles) change identities as they whiz through the universe. Neutrinos are the second most abundant particles in the universe after photons. Their chameleon-like nature shows that they oscillate from one type to another, dispelling the notion that they are massless. Basically, when they come from the sun, they can undergo metamorphosis in the atmosphere. This will surely turn concepts about evolution upside down. At a particle level, metamorphosis is occurring, probably at speeds we cannot clock.

To me, all of this is truly amazing, interesting, and miraculous, but I don't need to understand it completely in order for it to encourage faith in what I cannot see. There is so much going on "in and around us," that we cannot see.

WHAT ABOUT PSYCHOLOGY?

As we look at the collective work of the notable minds across the field of psychology like Sigmund Freud, Carl Jung, Otto Rank, Soren Kierkegaard, and many others, we will see them tell us that we live under a spell of deception, that the "human condition" is the battle of the conscious mind employing tactics to repress the reality of existence. They call this neurosis, or sin, while through the subconscious, we get half-glimpses of the true reality.

The obvious issue would be the fundamental anxiety around impermanence: we are running out of time; we are going to physically die. This, of course, is well documented as a part of the "general neurosis," and perhaps if death was all we had to reconcile with, we could focus on living with zest and making the most of every moment. As Solomon said, "Eat, drink, and be merry."

The paradox is that deeper than the fear of death, and what we so diligently work to repress, is our "absolute knowledge" about the truth of our miraculous existence. To quote Dr. Ernest Becker from his book *Denial of Death*, "And what is this fear, but a fear of the reality of creation in relation to our powers and possibilities."

Psychologist Rudolph Otto said about this intuitive knowledge we all have, "Most of us by the time we leave childhood—have repressed our vision of the primary miraculousness of creation. We have closed it off, changed it, and no longer perceive the world as it is to raw experience. Sometimes we may recapture this world by remembering some striking childhood perceptions…"

Otto Rank talked about "the terror of the world, the feeling of overwhelming awe, wonder and fear in the ace of creation—the miracle of it."

The brilliant psychologist Abraham Maslow talked about concepts like "full humanness," and "fear of one's own greatness." In his words, "We fear our highest possibility. We are generally afraid to become that which we glimpse in our most perfect moments… We enjoy and even thrill to the godlike possibilities we see in ourselves in such peak moments. And yet we simultaneously shiver with weakness, awe, and fear before these very same possibilities.

Maslow calls it the "Jonah syndrome." Freud calls it the "wrecked by success" syndrome. Otto Rank talked about it with no special name. In essence, the ego tells us we can't deal with the full intensity of life. We just can't handle ecstatic, delirious happiness, not for too long. "It's too much," the ego says. "I could die."

The "ego," our notion of separateness, the perpetuation of Satan's great lie, does not want to die a psychological death, allowing the real person to be born again to the salvation of truth.

To quote Jesus, "Truly, truly I say to you, unless one is born again, he cannot see the Kingdom of God." (John 3:13; New King James Version)

Truth:

> You and I are "individualizations" (undivided instances) of His spirit, and the Jonah Syndrome is "spiritual warfare."

Freud said, "Man lives by lying to himself about his world" and is hostile about admitting it. All of Freud's well-known theories of complexes (what the Bible calls abominations, jackals and serpents) tie back to this core problem of needing to cast a web of lies and delusions about reality.

Basically, we know it's there, but fear has us too overwhelmed to deal with it, so we try to block it out. This is called "neurosis," and is the lie cast by Satan that we are separated from God.

Psychoanalysis says that this "repression of truth as self (ego) protection is normal, because everyone has trouble living with the truth of existence." So the essence of human normality is the "refusal of reality" (living a lie). The human condition then (called fallen man), is that we are in a constant state of anxiety (fear) in which we are trying to figure out who we are, trying to reconcile the body to the "real self," while at the same time keeping the truth at bay, at all costs. This is called spiritual warfare.

Pascal says that, "Men are so necessarily mad, that to try not to be mad would amount to another form of madness."

Freud talked about "the lie." "I therefore maintain," said Freud, "the fear of death is to be regarded as an analogue of the fear of castration (being cut off), and the situation to which the ego (self) reacts is the state of being forsaken or deserted by the protecting superego (God) by the powers of destiny—which puts an end to the security against every danger.

So we avoid consciously thinking about existence, and we are busy casting lies about life to repress fear. How then does this "spiritual warfare" manifest itself in day-to-day life? What does it look like? Before I answer, let me point out that the aim of Satan's warfare is not just to distract the individual from awakening to the truth, but to squash his or her ability to affect change in humanity, to slow the spread of salvation.

Here is an example of how the lie about our existence and being cut off from God achieves its goal in spiritual warfare. Imagine that your wife is cheating on you (or your husband if you are a wife), and that in your denial (neurosis) you try to block it out, because the truth will alter everything, the security of a happy family, your hopes, dreams, and plans, the lives of your children, your day-to-day reality, resulting in the loss of the very salvation you thought you had found in "mattering," in having significance through the roles of husband, father, hero, provider, lover, and "man."

It is called "neurotic" (the Biblical term is "abomination.") Your misplaced efforts of narrowly trying to find salvation in a romantic relationship (worshiping a false idol) are being defeated. Perhaps now in trying to hold your marriage together, you become overly passive, catering to her every demand, becoming dependent and fearful of making your own life without her, no matter how poorly she treats you. Now, in a full-fledged co-dependent experience (a neurotic abomination), you experience guilt (being humbled and stopped in ways we don't understand), failure, panic, depression, and then loss of self.

Now you're even further away from your authentic self. You are spiritually dead (desolation).

Pearl said, "The ironic thing about the narrowing-down of neurosis is that the person (ego) seeks to avoid death, but he does it by killing off so much of himself."

We can follow this thread further and see devastation turn to annihilation when she continues to cheat and the husband relapses into the involuntary escape mechanism of alcoholism.

Now, for the cheating wife, spiritual warfare is no less damaging (nor are the effects on her children as they shape their beliefs about life and relationships). Although one might look to make her the villain, she struggles with the same fallen state, wrestles with confusion, perplexity, and conflict about where "she" really is in the inner self or her body. If the marriage was originally based on sex or material security alone, then their marital life is only an illusion of togetherness, a lie, a deception. In discovering this false union, she might then look for "true" satisfaction in secret. Acting out sexually might be looking for love, or be a subconscious effort to control the determinism of her life, or an involuntary escape mechanism, an addiction. Whether it's "narcissistic neurosis," "nymphomania," or some other collection of labels, whether she's disassociating from her body and it's a way to depersonalize and destroy intimacy, or whether she's seeking to lose her anxiousness, helplessness, and sense of separation through physical union, it is all self-destructive sin and it won't help her reconcile herself wholly. In fact, things get worse as she loses whatever feelings of salvation she had in the roles of good housewifery and motherhood. If this is just a small example of what the Bible calls spiritual warfare, we can see how subversive and effective a distraction it is.

Many of us may not go through dramatic, messy experiences like this example. On the other hand, the divorce rate is near 40%

in the United States, and I would imagine the infidelity rate is even higher, with all the sneaky behaviors that occur across Facebook and iPhones.

"They have made themselves crooked paths, whoever takes that way shall not know peace." (Isaiah 59:8 New King James Version)

I AM THAT I AM, who am I, am I trapped in this body or up in the sky?

The science of psychology says the "human condition" of living in a false reality of self-perpetuated fear and dishonesty, of suppressing our fear of being cut off and alone, fear of dying, and fears of the reality of creation, our powers and possibilities, and at living in a fractured state of confusion as to where the real "me" is—has only one salvation, full renunciation, "to renounce the world and oneself, to lay the meaning of it to the Power of Creation." The conclusion of the life work of the hard-headed, empirical psychologist, Otto Rank, a disciple of Freud and an expert on neurosis, was that "Man is a theological being," not a biological one. Rank says, "The need for a truly religious ideology… is inherent in human nature, and its fulfillment is basic to any kind of social life. One should reach for the highest beyond religion. Man should cultivate the passivity of renunciation of the highest powers, no matter how difficult it is. Anything less is less than full development, even if it seems like weakness and compromise to the best of thinkers."

Even with the majority of the psychiatric community, like mainstream society, misunderstanding the message of Christianity to be about passively waiting for the next life, their solution is to believe in what Christ taught.

Soren Kierkegaard gave his formula for the "ideal of mental health," the true essence of man. He called him "the knight of faith."

A man who lives in faith given over the meaning of life to his creator and lives centered on the energies of his maker. He is fully in the world on its terms and wholly beyond the world in his trust of the invisible dimension." Norman Brown wrote in his *Life Against Death*: "If we can imagine an unexpressed man—a man strong enough to live and therefore strong enough to die, and what no man has ever been, an individual—such a man would have… overcome guilt and anxiety (fear)… In such a man would be fulfilled on earth the mystic hope of Christianity, the resurrection of the body, in a form, as Luther said, free from death and filth… with such a transfigured body the human soul can be reconciled, and the human ego could become once more what it was designed to be in the first place, a body ego…"

In his book, *In Search of Self*, C. F. Miller said, "The healthy person, the true individual, the self-realized soul, the "real" man, is the one who has transcended himself." Pearl says, "The ego must be brought down to nothing in order for self-transcendence to begin." Maslow talked about "being cognition," "full humanness," and the "actualization of self" in terms of awe, splendor, sense of one's free inner expansion, and the miracle of being.

Otto Rank agreed with Soren Kierkegaard when he said, "The sinner (neurotic) is hyperconscious of the very thing he tries to deny… The more he separates and inflates himself, the more anxious he becomes. Sin and neurosis are two ways of talking about the same thing—the complete isolation of the individual, his disharmony with the rest of nature, his attempt to create his own world from within himself [ego]." Carl Jung said, "egocentricity, as a mode of being possessed, is an 'autonomous complex' (evil spirit) blind to the larger dimensions of the self." Kierkegaard talked about the self-created man (or person), one who tries to become his/her own god and plunges "into the distractions of great undertakings, he/she will seek forgetfulness in sensuality, perhaps in debauchery…" He says that at its extreme, defiant "self-creation" can become demonic. A "demonic rate," when carried to the extreme, is observed in the demonic possession of beings like Hitler.

I (in Greek), "the ego" have been crucified with Christ, and it is no long I (the ego) who live, but it is Christ who lives in me (the true self). And the life I (ego) now live in the flesh, I live by faith in the Son of God who loved me and gave himself for me. (Galatians 2:29-2 New King James Version)

Earlier I talked about there being entities outside of us that also create evil, so it's not only the oppressed or possessed self that we must relinquish, but also the false systems of thought we have been raised on. In his book, *The Powers That Be*, Walker Wink, humanitarian, theologian, and professor of Biblical Interpretation, expressed this well. I'm paraphrasing him, but in effect he said, we must also relinquish the outer network of beliefs that we have internalized, the systems, powers and institutions that have socialized us into falsehood (hatred, racism, materialism, false Christianity, etc.) He said, "Rationalists must [relinquish] the idolatry of the mind, dominating personalities to their power, and proud achievers to their accomplishments."

…"In the cross of our Lord Jesus Christ by which the world (socialized systems of falsehood) has been crucified to me, and I to the world." (Galatians 6:14. New King James Version)

In his conclusion Rank said, "Psychology as self-knowledge is self-deception… if neurosis is sin, and not disease, then the only thing which can 'cure' it… the only way the neurotic can come out of isolation is to become a part of the larger wholeness as religion (Christianity) has always represented.

"For everyone who has been born of God overcomes the world. And this is the victory that has overcome the world (society and the lies it teaches)—our faith (belief that what Jesus taught is the truth)." …"We know that we are from God, and the whole world lies in the power of the evil one." (1 John 5:4, 19, New King James Version)

Truth: We are all liars, we all sin, have misplaced guilt, and secretly struggle with our identity and ego. There is no salvation in romance, no reconciling ourselves wholly through casual sex, and no fabricated storyboard of life that will bring security and inner peace, none! Regardless of how well you try to behave or how "neat" you try to make your life look, there's only one way out, and that's for the truth to be heard, seen, and understood in your conscious mind. The spell has to be broken, the illusion dissolved, and the mind reborn to the truth of who you are as a spiritual being, a son or daughter of God.

When we read the Bible (which was translated into English) and get the idea that the meaning might not be what it seems to literally say—e.g. "hand" is not talking about the physical part of our bodies attached to the arm, we are right—not because the Bible was written in symbolic code, but because the translation into the English language took terms speaking about man's thoughts, beliefs, and states of consciousness and converted them into English words that are largely concrete. The original Hebrew terms might speak directly and literally about thoughts dispatched from God being delivered to us, that once conceived in our minds, will change our false beliefs, allowing us to take negative thoughts captive and renew our minds, overcoming fear. Translated into English, these words suggest a concrete story about man, his enemies, angels, then evildoers and darkness, leaving our minds to wrestle with what each of these things might symbolize.

The whole of the Bible is teaching us how to live out the Truth of our being as described in Genesis, as the expressions of God's Spirit, who have dominion over conditions.

Let's look at what the Bible says about you and me.

OUR EXISTENCE AND THE NATURE OF OUR BEING: GENESIS 1-3

Many people reading the Bible have breezed through the beginning of Genesis and miss God explaining what we are, who we really are. If we did read it, it probably didn't make sense. Looking through our filters (the lies of this world, how society has indoctrinated us), it would be hard to contemplate, much less grasp what is being said, since it so different from how we see ourselves.

With an understanding of the ancient Middle East, Hebrew grammar, and correct prepositions, scholars today know that Genesis 1:26 states that God made us "**as**" His image, as the traditional translation suggests. So we are not something kind of like or resembling God, but are literally the living images of God's Spirit on earth, like Jesus was when He was manifested as a man. We are meant to be vessels that express, reflect, and magnify God's Spirit. The Hebrew term translated into the English word "image" means and the one assigned to "likeness" comes from the root word meaning "to magnify."

The implication here is that in actuality, we are individualizations of God's spirit, not just creatures that have moral, ethical, and intellectual abilities. When we become aware of this truth, then we can operate as Divine Spirit too. When we operate as designed (think and believe), we are the lightbulbs, and He's the electricity!

In Genesis 3, God describes to us "the lie" and the identity crisis, so to speak, that Adam spawned for mankind in having the false realization of being separated from God. Man became "self-conscious," instead of God-conscious.

At this point, it might be easier to see that the whole of the Bible is talking about changing that "consciousness" back to God, literally shedding selfishness, the ego, and becoming "selfless," our true identity in Christ.

GOD COMMUNICATING WITH MAN ABOUT OUR TRUE IDENTITY

Now let's jump to the first time God reveals Himself to Moses. Read the following passages as you normally would.

> **Exodus 3:4-13**
>
> 4 So when the LORD saw that he turned aside to look, God called to him from the midst of the bush and said, "Moses, Moses!"
>
> And he said, "Here I am."
>
> 5 Then He said, "Do not draw near this place. Take your sandals off your feet, for the place where you
> stand *is* holy ground." 6Moreover He said, "I *am* the God of your father — the God of Abraham, the God of Isaac, and the God of Jacob." And Moses hid his face, for he was afraid to look upon God.
>
> 7 And the LORD said: "I have surely seen the oppression of My people who *are* in Egypt, and have heard their cry because of their taskmasters, for I know their
> sorrows. 8So I have come down to deliver them out of the hand of the Egyptians, and to bring them up from that land to a good and large land, to a land flowing with milk and honey, to the place of the Canaanites and the Hittites and the Amorites and the Perizzites
> and the Hivites and the Jebusites. 9Now therefore, behold, the cry of the children of Israel has come to Me, and I have also seen the oppression with which

> the Egyptians oppress them. [10]Come now, therefore, and I will send you to Pharaoh that you may bring My people, the children of Israel, out of Egypt."
>
> [11]But Moses said to God, "Who *am* I that I should go to Pharaoh, and that I should bring the children of Israel out of Egypt?"
>
> [12]So He said, "I will certainly be with you. And this *shall be* a sign to you that I have sent you: When you have brought the people out of Egypt, you shall serve God on this mountain."
>
> [13]Then Moses said to God, "Indeed, *when* I come to the children of Israel and say to them, 'The God of your fathers has sent me to you,' and they say to me, 'What *is* His name?' what shall I say to them?"

Now read it again, paying close attention to the exchange between God and Adam. What is God trying to get Adam to see? What spiritual truth is God communicating to Man?

Here's a clue: whenever someone says, "I am," regardless of what follows, they are always making an affirmative statement about their identity, or some aspect of it. Conversely, when they ask, "am I?," regardless of what follows, they are questioning their identity or some aspect of it. What you claim through I AM statements, no one else can do for you or to you. As you declare "I AM," you are initiating the power of dominion and creation, producing every condition, circumstance, or event in your life.

God's dialogue with Moses is about his identity in connection to God. It can be difficult to see this pattern in some English-speaking Bibles because translators, not catching the importance of word placement in these cases, made the stylistic choice to reorder the "AM Is" to "I AMs," theoretically making it smoother to read.

In Verse 3:4, God calls Moses, "Moses, Moses!" He replies, "Here AM I."

As the dialogue progresses, God tells Moses, "I AM the God of your Father..." Then in Verse 3:11, Moses asks God, "Who AM I that I should go to the "chief idea of limitation" (the Pharaoh) and deliver the "ideas that God will rule" (the children of Israel) out of limitation (Egypt)? Moses asks "What shall I say to them (the children of Israel)?" Then God says to Moses in Verse 14, "I AM THAT I AM," and tells him to say, "I AM sent me to you."

The dialogue continues through Exodus, with Moses doubting that he has the credibility and power to accomplish the tasks. Then God guides him to realize the "I AM," the Indwelling Spirit (YHWH, "I AM" in English).

By getting Moses to switch to the voice of the first person, getting him to say the affirmative "I AM," he is claiming that he is realizing at some level that he is connected to God, "I am that." Then the power of God can work through him.

God is telling man how to have dominion over the earth, earth being expression or manifestation on the physical plane.

This is key to prayer, to our spiritual development. By saying I AM THAT and thinking about God's spirit inside of us, we are kicking off the mental dialogue. We are automatically working on the realization of the Presence of God within us, thus overcoming "the lie" or working out our salvation.

In Verse 15, God said to Moses, "Thus you shall say to the children of Israel: "The Lord (Yahweh) God (Elohim) of your fathers... has sent me to you. This is my name forever and this is my memorial to all generations..." Moses says, the I AM is my nature as a being forever, his identity as a channel for God's power to flow through.

Now that you are aware that God is talking to man about our identity, you will read the Bible differently; you will see this dialogue between God and man repeated as He calls someone into ministry and they are unclear about their identity. The scripture and prayers you read will make more sense to your conscious mind.

We can see this dialogue between God and man repeated in the Old Testament as He calls someone into ministry and they are unclear about their identity:

- Genesis 22:11: But the Angel of the Lord called to him from heaven and said, "Abraham, Abraham!" So he said, "Here am I."
- 1 Samuel 3:4: "...the Lord called Samuel (to ministry as a child), and he answered "Here am I."
- 2 Chronicles 2:6: Solomon saying, "who am I then that I should build Him a temple..."
- Job 9:32: Job, claiming his identity says, "I am that."
- Isaiah 6:8: When God is calling him into ministry, saying "Here am I."
- Etc., etc.

Now let's take what we've just learned and read from the point when God calls Isaiah to ministry and on through the prophecy of Jesus. When Isaiah is called to become a prophet in chapter 6, we can see the same identity dialogue between God and man. God says, "whom shall I send..." and in Verse 8, Isaiah, wanting to help, responds with, "Here I am..."

We're not going to focus on 6:9 - 7:13, but between those verses there's more dialogue through prophecies related to the Syro-Ephaiarite wars in Syria and the invasion of Judah, spiritually about man's wrong thought under the deception of "the lie" vs. right thought, the Truth, God's holy ideas.

We resume focus again at Verse 7:14 with the prophecy of Jesus: "Behold the virgin shall conceive and bear a son, and shall call His name God is with us (Immanuel)." In other words, the soul that looks to God alone will conceive the spiritual idea that God is with us, that His spirit dwells within us. Then if we skip back to 9:6 again, we can reread the spiritual ideas of Jesus, being the light that exposes the Truth to us, that the full power of God resides in us, and we can rely on that indwelling spirit to guide us to perfect peace.

Now we can start to see this "I AM" dialogue throughout the Bible: "Most assuredly I say to you, before Abraham was I AM" (John 8:58), or in the Book of Joel (the Lord is God), "then you shall know that I AM in the midst of Israel (the spiritual idea of Christ): I AM the Lord your God and there is no other."

My people (believers) shall never be put to shame. In other words, God, the indwelling spirit can be found in the spiritual idea of Christ, that indwelling Power is your God and Savior, and there is no other. Believers in this Truth will never pale (be disappointed, ashamed), or Job saying, "I AM THAT," in 9:32.

THE MEANING OF JESUS'S NAME

I became a Christian late in life, but I was pretty passionate about it, so initially, when I started praying out loud and saying, "In Jesus's name we pray," I conceptualized my acknowledgment of God's greatness, my trust in Him, and a humble request to join Him spiritually. So saying His name had meaning to me.

But once I started studying the Bible and looked at the significance of a "name," a bright light went on. How can we do something "in His name" without first being clear on what His name stands for?

The "**name**" of anything in the Bible stands for its nature and character, but when we read things like, "gathered in My Name," "call on My Name," "in the name of the Lord," "in God's name," and "in the name of Jesus," we frequently take that at face value, without **thinking** about what that name means, leaving us with a surface-level understanding of what we're reading or saying.

While it is surely useful to verbally say the name of Jesus during our prayer, its value is not that the God out there somewhere is pleased at our obedience (not that He isn't), but rather that we are thinking about God, His nature, and His character, which means we are thinking about ourselves in relation to God, too. Now, by saying God's name, we are consciously thinking about Him on some level, and that cues our subconscious to think about Him on a deeper level, which is great.

As an aside, I want to point out something about God's instruction and reading scripture. God says, "So shall My word be that goes forth from My mouth. It shall not return to Me void, but shall accomplish what I please, and it shall prosper in the thing for which I sent it." (Isaiah, 55:11). When we read a story in the Bible, we should be conscious that we are receiving instruction from God at that moment. We might, for example, read where God gives Isaiah some instruction, who in turn passes that instruction on to others. What we might not realize is that scripture is designed to have the same effect on us. Since God knows the human mind, He knows that by reading the word "I," we subconsciously switch into the first person.

We'll see how powerful this is later, as we look at specific prayers, meditations, and affirmations He has given us to use, but I wanted to make mention of it in the context of "I AM."

SO WHAT DOES THE BIBLE SAY THE NATURE OF GOD IS?

According to Jesus, man misinterprets scripture, perverting its meaning and creating a distorted notion of God. So first we need to get clear on what Jesus says the correct notion of God's nature is. As a refresher, God is Spirit itself, love itself, intelligence itself, creativity itself. He has no limitation and can overcome any circumstance or change any condition. Jesus also explicitly corrects man's false notion of God, pointing out that He is nonviolent, not a killer, does not oppress, dominate, nor force His will on others. He is not racist, sexist or classist, loves "all" of mankind, and does not express favoritism.

Most Christmas pageants tell the story of Jesus's birth by reciting some combination of verses from Isaiah in the Old Testament and Matthew or Luke in the New Testament, which collectively tell the prophecy of the Son called Immanuel, "**God with us,**" being conceived and born to a virgin, and then the fulfillment of that prophecy with Mary giving birth to Jesus.

Many non-Christians would recognize, "Behold, the virgin shall conceive and bear a son, and shall call his name Immanuel," and "Unto us a child is born," as Bible verses referencing the birth of Jesus. A lot of Christians haven't gone far past that ourselves and have a fairly limited view of the meaning of "virgin" and the spiritual significance of "a child is born."

While the Bible tells historically accurate stories, the purpose in telling them is instruction on spiritual truths. Spiritual things and mental concepts are not concrete, so they must always be described figuratively. This means that understanding the symbolism used in the Bible is pretty important if we want to consciously grasp what God is communicating. Otherwise, it will seep in gradually over time (perhaps years) through our subconscious. To interpret means to "open up," to "unravel."

ISAIAH 7:14

We're going to get into symbolism a bit more later, but in the Bible a child symbolizes a **spiritual idea** and a virgin stands for the **soul that looks to God alone**. The son is the builder of **your identity**. The soul is always referenced as feminine. So, "Behold, the virgin shall conceive and bear a son, and shall call His name Immanuel," means **"The soul that looks to God alone will conceive the spiritual idea that God is with us,"** that His spirit dwells within us.

The Prophecy of Jesus's Birth and the Significance of His Name - Isaiah 9:2 and 9:6

9:2
"The people who walked in darkness
Have seen a great light;
Those who dwelt in the land of the
Shadow of death,
Upon them a light has shined."

9:6
"For unto us a child is born
Unto us a Son is given;
And government will be upon
His shoulder.
And His name will be called
Wonderful, Counselor, Mighty God
Everlasting Father, Prince of Peace."

This poem is meant to be read as a meditation. Read each statement and pause, contemplating its meaning in your life.

Now we'll read this looking at the compressed meaning, applying what we know of the symbolism used, and looking up some of the original Hebrew words used and their meaning from a concordance.

9:2
The people who walked in the darkness

Those under deception, those who believe "the lie," who think they're alone, who worry.

Have seen a great light;

Awakened to the Truth.

Those who dwelt in the land of the shadow of death;

The Bible speaks not of death, but the shadow, our "false belief;" our fear of death. These are people who suffer the death of hope, of joy, of self-respect. The heartbroken, the tired, the sick, the depressed, the addicted, the afflicted, etc.

9:6
"For unto us a child is born, unto us a Son is given;

A spiritual idea is born to our soul — conceived into our minds.

And the government will be upon His Shoulder.

The burden will rest on Him. You don't have to figure it all out, you can turn your problems, sickness, and worry over to him. You will no longer have to manage life alone.

And His name will be called.

The characteristics that make Him up will be…

Wonderful,

Pele, a miracle, performs wondrous things. The correct Hebrew term is miraculous. When this spiritual idea is born into your consciousness, the miracle will come into your life.

Counselor,

You can trust Him to guide your life, He is never mistaken.

Mighty God

Gibbor'el
Powerful Almighty

Everlasting Father,

ad. eternal/ab. Father
This establishes our relationship to Jesus. He is our Father, provider, creator and protector.

Prince of Peace

Sar; head, chief, captain/Shalowm; Perfect health, Prosperity. He can bring perfect peace to your soul, teaching you things beyond your current understanding.

THE SPIRITUAL IDEA OF THE SON

John 3:16 is one of the most widely known Bible verses, but it is probably one of the least studied. It seems simple enough to understand.

> "For God so loved the world that He gave His only begotten Son, that whoever believes in Him should not perish but have everlasting life."

We are instructed to study scripture, to meditate on it day and night, and to pray for understanding. There are good reasons for this beyond being a religious fanatic. The revelation from God to man—the spiritual teaching in the Bible, our instructions for operating as designed—these are about our thoughts and states of consciousness, not about physical, concrete, non-spiritual things. We are not being told about events that occurred so we can know history. **We are being taught about ourselves.** Study of scripture for English-speaking believers is that much more necessary since it was originally written in ancient Hebrew and Greek which didn't separate the spiritual from the physical. They were viewed as the inner and outer aspects of something. And the translation into English often resulted in the compression of deep terms into fairly generic English words, which, by the way, we frequently "assume" to know the meaning of.

The first several times I **read** John 3:16, it never crossed my mind that it was talking about you and me and our identity. It pretty plainly was speaking about Jesus. When I **studied** it, I was amazed. First, we look at the context of the story and see that Jesus is talking to a Jewish religious leader about those born of the spirit being "born again." Jesus tells him, "Most assuredly, I say to you, unless one is born again, he cannot see the Kingdom of Heaven." We've already reviewed in the previous pages that the Kingdom of Heaven is within us, that we were born of God's Spirit, and that the birth of a child refers to the birth of a spiritual idea in us. With this information setting the stage, we now go to our concordance to look up the entire passage to make sure we really understand it.

John 1:1-5 summarizes the situation again: "In the beginning was the Word, and was with God, and the **Word was God**…" "All things were made through Him, and without Him nothing was made that was made. In Him was life, and the life was the light of **men**. And the light shines in the darkness, and **the darkness did not comprehend it."** The **Word** (*logos* in Greek) was used to denote **the creative energy that generated the universe**, and the Word is Jesus, and Jesus is God. "He is the image of the invisible God (Colossians 1:15), the exact representation of God's character (see Hebrews 1:3).

Christ entered this world of deception of "darkness" to give it spiritual light, but society could not comprehend. This is the same situation today.

Original Greek Terms Used - Keywords

> "For ***Theos*** so ***agapo*** the ***kosmos*** that he ***didomi*** His ***monogenes hulos*** so that whoever ***pisteau*** in Him should not ***apollumi***, but have everlasting ***zoe***."

How it reads when rendered directly as written:

> **"For God so loved the arrangement of creation that He brought forth the Source Idea from which we derive our identity, that whoever has faith in Him should not fully separate, but have eternal spiritual life [remain connected to God forever]."**

God (*Theos*)
Love (*agapo*) befriended
Gave (*didomi*) brought forth
Only begotten (*monogenes*) remaining, from root "source" or cause"
Son (*hulos*) son, from Hebrew Ben, "builder of family name," i.e., "identity."
World (*kosmos*) arrangement, decoration
Believes (*pisteuo*) to have faith, faith being the evidence (Hebrews 11:1-3)
Life (*zoe*) spiritual existence, awareness of connection to God
Perish (*apollumi*) fully separate, depart

Believing in Christ *Pisteuo* - "faith in a person," "to entrust to," from *pisto*, "accept as truth," and *pistos*, "trustworthiness:" The belief that God manifests Himself as a man, Jesus, and of course that He died and was resurrected; AND that He told us the "truth" about His nature as God, and our existence as spiritual children of God; AND that He modeled all aspects of right living for us to follow, how to live, love, and relate to God and our fellows; AND that as a man He lived and died sacrificially upholding the integrity of God's holy, righteous ideals, and proving to us His love and trustworthiness.

Salvation "*Ysuwah*" the Hebrew word that means "Jesus," saved, health, welfare, deliverance; *Soteria* - rescue, save, health, deliver: Because you believe that all which Christ said and did was "truth," you know that in reality you are not alone, that God, your spiritual Father, in fact provides everything that you need, spiritual nourishment, food, shelter, protection and people to share love with. As you place your trust in this, you experience both the peace of turning your burdens over to God, and the provisions and blessings that miraculously flow into your daily life, but as you start to align with your divine purpose, you realize that life is truly about expressing unselfish love. Salvation is overcoming the sense of separation from God. It's the realization of God's presence, that you are connected to Him, the increased awareness that His spirit is truly a part of you. You practice turning yourself over to Him so that He can live in your thoughts and acts, so that He can inhabit you.

In the Bible, the word "interpretation" means to "unravel" or "untie." When we look at the words "know," "knowledge," "understanding," etc. and the various terms they were translated from, we see "wide-open eyes at something remarkable," to "get it," "putting things together," to "comprehend," and when we look at the idea of waiting for God's judgment, we see that most of the terms having to do with impending judgment, justice, or punishment are in reference to waiting for the cumulative effect of "right principle" being applied or not, and the circumstances of conditions (a.k.a. consequences of blessings, etc.) will follow right or wrong thoughts and states of consciousness.

Jesus is not God's "only" Son. Rather, he is the spiritual idea of the "Son," and all that it teaches and stands for as modeled by Jesus to man, which is the cause, the source of humanity's true identity. God manifests "Himself" as Jesus to teach us about our true identity as the sons of God. He came as "the Son" to model the correct parent-child relationship we are to have with Him.

When we get it, when we understand, we follow the spiritual idea [obeying], and are God's sons and daughters, the images, and expressions of his spirit. When we believe this and all the Son taught, we are saved, because we are never again separated from God. We know the truth!

Let's continue on with John, Chapter 3 for a few verses, looking for the spiritual meaning. As we do think about what you've learned of symbolism, things you've learned in general from Christ's teachings, think about the dialogue between God and Moses about Moses's identity, what we've learned about the Indwelling Spirit, the I AM and the meaning of "the Son's" name, the Child's name, Jesus's name.

Read the verses 3:17-21 below, in which I have replaced the key English words with the original Greek terms used according to *Strong's Concordance*, and see if it makes sense to you. See if it connects to the foundational dialogue between God, in various forms, and man, about the truth of our identity and how salvation comes to those who come to understand this idea, "the Son," and believe in it.

Jesus continues to explain to Nicodemus, a Pharisee, ruler of the Jews, "the light," the Spiritual idea of "the Son" as man's true identity, the concept of being "born again," and the Indwelling Spirit as the means of preserving and protecting man as created (helping us to operate as designed).

Read both the English Standard Version and the exercise I did in replacing the English words with the original Greek terms used and see what your thoughts are.

<u>English Standard Version</u>
"For God did not send His Son into the world to condemn the world, but in order that the world might be saved through him." (John 3:17 English Standard Version)

<u>Study Exercise - Authors Rendering</u>
"For God sent the Spiritual idea of our identity into the world, into our thoughts—to decide mentally for or against the arrangement of creation but in order that it might be preserved through that idea (knowledge of the Indwelling Spirit, Christ in me, the I AM). John 3:17 (exercise).

The difference for me personally in reading the plain English version and studying these verses for spiritual meaning is not so much about correct vs. incorrect interpretation as it is about my perception of God, i.e., the tone of the dialogue, as well as the depth and clarity of my understanding of what's being communicated.

In comparison, if I just read the English version, I am not thinking about "my" identity. I am not thinking of myself as a son of God, but the focus is on "Jesus as the only son." I also detect a harshness; it seems like God's tone is judgmental. I assume the word "condemnation" to mean judgment with impending negative consequences; the words "evil" and "wicked" to speak of people who are bad and corrupt at their core, people who love evil.

When I study the original words, I see that in fact the dialogue is an understanding, caring, loving one. God talks about the deception many are under and how the decisions they make "not" to follow man's operating instructions (not to obey) comes from a place of emotional anguish, pain, and spiritual emptiness, not from depravity, worthlessness, or a "bad" and corrupt nature. In essence, He's stating that the ego (the us under the spell of the lie) does not want to be exposed as a lie; the ego does not want to die, allowing us to be born again without it. What are the differences for you?

<u>English Standard Version</u>
"And this is the judgment: the light has come into the world, and people loved the darkness rather than the light because their works were evil." (John 3:19 English Standard Version).

<u>Study Exercise - Authors Rendering</u>
"And the decision was made (by God) to manifest from rays into the world the truth (to bring forth Jesus to expose, teach, and model our truth), and all the harmful thoughts man thinks and speaks despite being exposed for "the lies" that they are—ideas coming from a place of emotional pain, anguish, and spiritual starvation." (John 3:19 exercise).

"For all the individuals who operate under the spell of deception (Satan's lie about God and us), hate the light and do not come to the light, the realization of God, the Truth, the spiritual idea of the Son, lest their deeds be exposed." (John 3:20 exercise).

<u>English Standard Version</u>
"But whoever does what is true comes to the light, so that it may be clearly seen that his works have been carried out in God." (John 3:21 English Standard Version).

<u>Study Exercise - Authors Rendering</u>
"But whoever follows the operating instructions comes to realize the idea of Jesus and the Indwelling Spirit (the light) and his deeds are clearly seen as things made manifest through God, thoughts carried out in God." (John 3:21 exercise).

<u>English Standard Version</u>
"Whoever believes in Him is not condemned, but whoever does not believe is condemned already, because he has not believed in the name of the only Son of God. (John 3:18 ESV, New King James Version)

<u>Study Exercise – Authors Rendering</u>
"Whoever has faith (evidence of what is not seen) in that idea (in Jesus) is not closed off, but whoever does not possess faith has already decided, is closed-minded even now, because he has not believed in the character and nature of His name, (see Isaiah 9:6), the source idea from where mankind (you and I) derives His true identity. (John 3:18 exercise).

THE BIBLICAL CONCEPT OF FAITH

People most often confuse faith with hope. The term "faith" in the Bible does not refer to **blind faith**, but actually to the **proof** that what God promises about existence is the truth, demonstrated by those who spiritually understand. Faith is a continuum.

> "Faith is the substance of things hoped for, the **evidence** of things Not seen. For by it elders obtained a good report." (Hebrews 11:1-3)

The truth is written on our hearts, so as young children we know, but as we get socialized, we forget and repress it.

In John 4:46-54, we see a nobleman ask Jesus to heal his son. In verse 50, it says the nobleman "believed" that Jesus could heal his son, but believing that Jesus can heal is not enough to save. It wasn't until after his son was healed that the nobleman truly believed Jesus was supernatural and put his faith in him, thus receiving salvation.

Jesus says, "Unless you people see signs and wonders, you will by no means believe." (John 4:48, New King James Version).

A **promise** from God is not a personal commitment, it's a statement about a precept, law, or statute that applies to man as the image and likeness of God's spirit. His laws are also ours. They are inherent to our nature, too. When we do not understand, and follow our operating instructions to express God, we function in error (sin).

"Faith is proof that what God said in the Bible is the absolute truth, the demonstration of results produced through prayer. The elders, those spiritually mature, trained believers, have obtained that evidence by understanding and correctly applying the principles." (Hebrews 11:1-3, Authors rendering, as written in Greek).

This success in seeing results from prayer (applying God's principles) increases faith from the size of a "mustard seed" to that which can "move mountains." We see this in the seemingly small confirmations of something we've prayed about and in the more obvious proof points, such a physical healing.

Key: When we start to understand and believe that the teachings and promises in the Bible are really "principles of our existence," "spiritual truths," "laws inherent to our very nature as beings,"—that they are the consequences that will always follow certain thoughts and states of consciousness—we gain the conviction to work at correctly applying those principles, in turn producing more evidence, increasing our faith.

Testimony: The dialogue in scripture around testimony has to do with seeing, hearing, and remembering the record of what God has done. Keeping the testimony means repeating it. It means seeing, hearing, or remembering and then declaring it with expectancy to produce the same miracle again in a different situation.

In the Bible, we are told that we are "saved by faith, not works," but also that "faith without works is dead." This is because it is understanding and applying the principles God teaches us, which change all of our unharmonious conditions, and doing those "works" produces evidence (faith).

When we exercise faith, we work as designed with dominion to express God on earth, "spreading His reign" and "producing fruit."

Jesus demonstrates this understanding in applying the power of thought in producing evidence (faith) by causing a fig tree to wither. When the disciples marveled at this miracle, Jesus said, "Truly, I say to you, if you have faith and do not doubt, you will not only do what has been done to the fig tree, but even if you say to this mountain, 'Be taken up and thrown into the sea,' it will happen" (Matthew 21:21, English Standard Version). And whatever you ask for in Prayer, you will receive, if you have faith.

By faith we understand that the universe was created by the word of God, so that what is seen was not made from things that are visible." (Hebrews 11:3, New King James Version). It was made out of prayers.

I cannot underscore this enough—the revelation from God to man—the spiritual teaching in the Bible, our instructions for working as designed, are about our "thoughts" and "states of consciousness," not about physical, concrete, non-spiritual things. Thoughts come first; then from them, physical conditions are manifest.

"A disciple is not above his Teacher, but everyone, when fully trained, will be like his Teacher (like Christ)." (Luke 6:40, New King James Version)

Picking up at 14:25-31, we read that between 3:00 am-6:00 am (the fourth watch of the night), Jesus went to His disciples, walking on the sea. They thought he was a ghost and cried out in fear. Jesus spoke to them, saying, "Be of good cheer! It is I, do not be afraid." ('It is I,' correctly rendered is "I AM.") Peter answered Him, "Lord, if it is you, command me to come to You on water." Jesus did and so Peter got out of the boat and started walking on the water towards Jesus, but when he saw the turbulent wind, he was afraid and began to sink. The teaching then goes like this: God can work miracles, focused on the "I AM." His spirit dwells in us. We too can do things that seem impossible. When we take our eyes off the I AM, when we lose focus on the indwelling spirit, we will have doubt, fear, and difficulty. And when this happens, we simply need to refocus on our belief that He can and will save us, ask for His hand (the power of thought), and fear will leave. The winds and stormy sea (our emotions) will calm.

It is the Christ nature in man that allows God to work through us. It is that nature that we want to cultivate. Jesus said, "I AM the way, and the truth and the life. No one comes to the Father except through Me (except through "the spectral idea of the Son, "the Indwelling spirit) (John 14:6, New King James Version)

Let's take a minute to look at how scripture works: as we read it consciously, the words masterfully invoke change in our consciousness. It uses a combination of poetry, symbolism, and switching in and out of the first person to work through our subconscious, bringing us to think about and realize our true identity; it causes us to say, "I AM" in the affirmative. As you seek or pray for understanding, glimpses of your intuition (absolute knowledge of truth) magnify and gradually you gain a clearer, more definitive sense of the presence of God, the Indwelling spirit, the I AM.

Key: If you wish to understand what Jesus, the Apostles, and the prophets were communicating, you will need to become a student (disciple) who works to become fully trained.

Let's look again at Matthew 21:19-22, with the mindset of understanding it spiritually. We must not "assume" meaning based on our notion of the English words used, since they were frequently translated from many different Greek and Hebrew terms into a single, common English word.

"Truly I say to you, if you have FAITH (which we now know involves understanding, and the application of statutes or principles through prayer, which produces proof) and do not DOUBT (*diakrino*: to separate thoroughly, withdraw; waiver), you will not only do what has been done to the fig tree (exercise dominion over living things), but also, if you say to the MOUNTAIN (there are several Greek words which have been translated into the English word "mountain," and they have a range of meanings such as "to pour upon," to "stimulate," or "provoke," or an "outcry.") The one used in this verse is *opheleon*, "I ought" in the first person, from *airo*, meaning "to take up," or "to raise." This is the uplifted consciousness ("in prayer"), "be taken up and thrust into the sea" (the sea from the root word of salt, symbolizing the soul), it will happen (*ginomal*, to generate, to become). And whatever you ask (*aiteo*, beg for, call for, crave, desire) in prayer you will be given (it will become).

If you have faith, you will have dominion not only over living things, but also over yourself, raising your consciousness high toward the realization of God in you through prayer and thrusting that truth into your soul.

CONSCIOUS CONTACT WITH OUR SOURCE - PRAYER

Through the Bible, God provides us with very specific instructions about prayer. Loving God means obeying God, and to obey God we must have faith and belief. If we have "faith" as described above, we can truly obey by living as expressions of God. We can have proper dominion over our world "only" when we live a life grounded in prayer. Prayer is the "how to"—the method by which we change our state of consciousness about the indwelling spirit, and that is how God tells us we can access His power to change conditions, to heal, to cast out fear, etc.

To love God is to imitate Christ in thought and action, to pray to God as He did and change the world.

"If anyone's will is to do God's will, he will know whether the teaching is from God or whether I am speaking on my own authority." (John 7:17, New King James Version)

When we try to find solutions out of fear or perceived problems, we make vain attempts to impose "our will," and we fail. When we simply and confidently go mentally inward to the visualization/realization of God's spirit, we cannot fail. God cannot and will not leave or forsake us; our job is to believe and follow His instructions (obey).

Jesus said, "But when you pray, go into your closet (chamber, upper room, house), "inward to the place within" and shut the door…" (Matthew 6:6, New King James Version) In other words, turn your thoughts inward to the realization of the indwelling Spirit and block out all other thoughts. Raise your thoughts to the highest level that you can.

This was the spiritual teaching we saw earlier in Deuteronomy 18 as well, on "taking our thoughts captive" and "renewing our mind." Let's look at two other well-known scriptures illustrating the same teaching in Daniel 6 and Psalm 23, and a couple from Isaiah.

The translation from Old Testament Aramaic/Hebrew and New Testament Greek has often led to confusion and assumptions on our part. Lord, Yahweh, I AM, Jehovah, Elohim, and Jesus are words with the same meaning.

In English, God says to Moses, "I AM the Lord, And I appeared to Abraham, to Isaac, and to Jacob by the name of God Almighty (el Elohim), my name Jehovah (YHWH, Hayah, Yeheh, Yahweh, or

Yehovah) was not known to them. In other words, people knew there was an all-powerful God, but were not aware that God's spirit was in them.

Original term used in scripture, *Strong Concordance* #, meaning of the term:

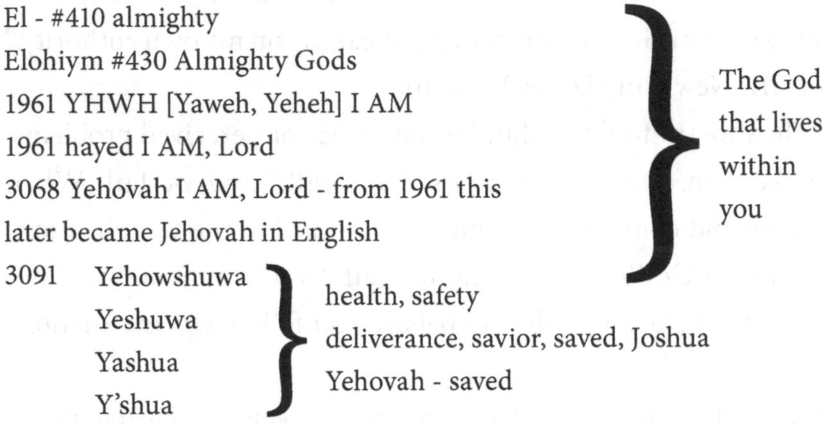

El - #410 almighty
Elohiym #430 Almighty Gods
1961 YHWH [Yaweh, Yeheh] I AM
1961 hayed I AM, Lord
3068 Yehovah I AM, Lord - from 1961 this
later became Jehovah in English
3091 Yehowshuwa
Yeshuwa
Yashua
Y'shua
health, safety
deliverance, savior, saved, Joshua
Yehovah - saved
The God
that lives
within
you

Iesous - Greek for 3091, later Jesus in English (Yeshuwa)

*NOTE: The English language had no "J" until the 1630s, after which Yehovah, Yeshua, and Iesous were translated as Jehovah and Jesus.

So God manifests Himself as a man to teach humanity about ourselves, existence, and His (God's) nature. As the prototype for true humanity, He modeled everything for us. Living as a human, Jesus experienced life as we do. He felt love, but He also went through rejection, betrayal, poverty, hunger, thirst, anger, temptation, injustice, and extreme pain at the hands of His fellows.

As a man, He received the Holy Spirit when He consecrated Himself to the Father's mission **as we are to do**. He demonstrated true love in acceptance of all who came to Him by working miracles to feed and heal, never rejecting anyone who asked for help, and He did it through Prayer with "absolute" belief and faith **as we are**

to do. He wasn't just showing us how magnificent God is, but how magnificent God's sons and daughters are, too. He was saying, "This is how we do it," "this is who we are," "this is what your family stands for," "this is how we love," "this is how you awaken your brothers and sisters to the truth of spiritual existence and Me." "This is how you Pray to bring harmony to the world."

Truly, Jesus expected you and me to be able to perform the same miracles He did. Jesus said, "Most assuredly I say to you, he who believes in Me (not just in My existence, but that all I say is truth), the works that I do, he will do also, greater works than these he will do, because I go to the Father (back to that role). And whatever you ask in my name, that I will do, that the Father may be glorified (honored) in the son (you and I). If you ask anything in my name, I will do it." (John 10:32) He didn't just expect that we "could" do the things He did, He expected that we "would" do them!... "He gave them power over unclean spirits, to cast out, and to heal all kinds of sickness, and all kinds of disease. He commanded… go, preach, saying, 'The kingdom of heaven is at hand,' Heal the sick, cleanse the lepers, raise the dead, cast out demons. Freely you have received, freely give." (John 10:7-8, New King James Version)

He didn't just expect that we would, but said that we did not believe in Him and didn't love Him unless we did these things. "Go into all the world and preach the gospel to every creature. He who believes and is baptized will be saved, but he who does not believe will be condemned. And these signs will follow those who believe: In My name they will cast out demons; they will speak in tongues (languages they had not previously known, enabling communication with all); they will take up serpents, and if they drink anything deadly, it will by no means harm them; they will lay hands on the sick and they will recover." (Mark 16:9-18, New King James Version)

"He who has My commandments (understands them) and keeps

them; it is he who loves Me. And I will love him and manifest Myself to Him."—John 14:21, New King James Version).

If you abide (live) in Me and My words abide in you, you will ask what you desire and it shall be done for you." (John 15:3, New King James Version).

"Therefore, I say to you whatever things you ask when you pray, believe that you receive them, and you will have them. (Mark 11:24, New King James Version)

"If you can believe, all things are possible to him who believes." (Mark 9:23, New King James Version).

"These things I have spoken to you, that my joy may remain in you, and that your joy may be full." (John 15:11, New King James Version).

"Evident to all… for in doing this you will save both yourself and those who hear you." (1 Timothy 4:8, New King James Version).

We should continuously work at practicing prayer until we find a method that demonstrates results. Flinging a request into the air and being filled with doubt that God will receive and fulfill it is not effective and will lead to disappointment. By the way, Satan is the "prince of the air" (airwaves, radio, television, Facebook, etc.) God is not reached through the air.

Even if we understand Genesis 1 correctly, we will still struggle with acceptance of who we truly are. We will wrestle with spiritual warfare, doubt, denial, etc. However, it is critical that we continue to acknowledge and contemplate what the Bible says about our existence as Beings, as it is the foundation of our success/salvation—it is "obedience."

Let's look at this dynamic for a minute. We are repeatedly told by Jesus about false teachers, perversion, corruption, and manipulation of God's word, so we know that the doctrine of man is under the influence of "the lie," and will misrepresent the Truth.

There is no place for ambiguity of words or meaning, that is part of deception (darkness) perpetuating itself. Man (or should I say "men" within the Catholic church and Jewish religion) have done a masterful job of perverting God's teaching in the Old Testament to instill "passive Christianity," the sense that we are powerless, unworthy, and corrupt by nature, when in fact God tells us just the opposite.

Here are examples of what God says about you and me, and the laws inherent in our existence as Beings:

- "If you ask for anything in My name, I will do it" (John 14:14, New King James Version).
- "You can tell the mountain to move into the water and it will."
- "Is not it written in your law 'I said you are gods'?" (John 10;34, New King James Version).
- "Most assuredly, I say to you, he who believes in Me (what I taught) the works that I do, he will do also, and greater works than these he will do, because I go to the Father (back to heaven, back to that role). And whatever you ask in My name, that I will do, that the Father (God) may be glorified in the son (you and I are the sons and daughters now). If you ask for anything in My name, I will do it." [John 14:12-14, Authors rendering].

Jesus modeled for us our true relationship to God. He's the Father, we're the sons and daughters. He makes it "absolutely" clear that when we understand and know this Truth, "anything" we ask for in His name will occur. Here we see Jesus telling us in no uncertain terms, we are God's spiritual sons (ideas), as He was on earth, and we "are empowered" through His spirit that lives within to do great things. On almost every page of the Bible, we are being told this truth, and yet our interpretation and acceptance of this has been and continues to be influenced by "the lie."

"Whoever is not with Me, is against Me..." (Luke 11:23)

"Every kingdom divided against itself is laid waste, and a divided household falls (Luke 11:17). We cannot believe the truth and the lie.

Example: "Enter through the narrow gate." (Matthew 7:13-24)

Ancient Biblical languages are packed with compressed meaning, but it's not that difficult to understand, "if" you are willing to study it. Obviously, we would have to see the value in putting forth the effort. If you take the time to look up the meaning and root of every word as originally written in a concordance, you will start to see clearly what God is communicating, but honestly, most do not care enough to become students (disciples).

1. **Enter through (or by) the narrow gate:**
   Looking at the actual rendering of the Greek words translated into "narrow" and "gate" this reads: "squeeze through a crowd of afflicted thoughts and circumstances (the world's view) to a precise understanding of the Truth.

2. **...for wide is the gate and broad is the way**
   (broad, flat, and wide open is the world's view; a reality which can be falsely manipulated, molded, or shaped as we choose).

Chapter 6, page 141
that leads to destruction

(corruption of right thought and people, spiritual or physical death and destruction of the planet).
and many enter through it.
(many go that route in thinking and living their lives).
But small is the gate and narrow the road

(the path to living in understanding of truth is precise, there's no room for deviation; you are either on or off the path, thinking right or wrong, obediently or disobediently, **in a state of love or fear).**

That leads to life

(our salvation, harmony, peace, joy, eternal fellowship with Christ and each other — being creative expression of God's beauty).

OUR EXISTENCE AND IDENTITY:

So, you and I are miraculous spiritual beings whose purpose is to express our spiritual Father's creative holy, life-breathing ideas while we are in the world. All humans are our fallen (deceived) spiritual brothers and sisters, who are inherently good, and whom we love. We have been entrusted with the administration of harmony for all living creatures on earth, in the air, and in the sea. It's only when we awaken to this truth (the full message of Jesus) that we can tap into our transformational power through God, thus having dominion over ourselves, and then our surroundings. Once we awaken out of the false reality (are "reborn") our mission is to share this truth with all, use our spiritual gifts with God's power working through us, and restore harmony or peace, health and prosperity; the expression of Divine love. This sounds like your understanding of humans, your understanding of Christianity, right? Christians presumably live out Christ's teachings, right?

10

WHAT CHRISTIANITY IS MEANT TO BE – CONCLUSION

Church, the body of Christ

We looked at how religion can lead us astray when the church becomes an institution or a foundation of power that regulates faith, so now let's look at how Jesus modeled and instructed His followers "to be the church" in loving our fellows.

The word church used in the New Testament, *ekklesia*, means a "calling out." It is referring to gatherings or meetings of those who are called to follow Christ. This could be the assembling of souls for a large prayer or worship service, a potluck, a small group training for new believers about the gospel and Jesus's instructions or teachings about prayer. It's also referring to people coming together; the movement, the ministry of reconciliation; the unity of the members of the body of Christ doing life together, helping each other live out the teachings of Jesus in spreading God's love throughout the world, coming together to address each other's needs or problems. We are designed to live in community (see 1 Corinthians 12:1-30).

The spiritual truth talked about in Revelation is that if we believe "the lie," we have something to prove and we end up striving, performing, and trying to control outcomes. We end up attempting to take personal responsibility for the success of "our" church...for God's success. Our innocent desire to do well can quickly turn into performance and wanting approval, acceptance, and validation—a subversive desire for power in wanting to be a dynamic pastor, a polished worship leader or the leader of a "special" church.

Revelation 17 tells of one kind of church that sits down on the scarlet beast (the lie, self-reliance, performance, striving, the idea of personal power, selfishness), and then Revelation 19 talks about the **true church of Christ,** the one who sits down on the white horse (the truth, light, love: selflessness, unmerited grace, forgiveness, humility, unity, and total dependence on God).

"Now I could **comprehend** (saw - *eido*) **through the idea of higher thoughts, the gospel** (heaven – *ouranos*), and **seeing** (behold - *idou*) the **vessel of light that the calvary sits on** [white - *leukos*; hoirse - *hippos*). And he who **sits down on** (sat – *kathemai*) **Him** is **called forth** (called – *kaleo*) **to believe and trust in the truth** (faith – *pistos*) and **with equity, distinguishes** (righteousness – *dikaiosune*), **to be engaged in spiritual warfare** (makes war – *polemeo*)" - Revelation 19:11, author's literal translation.

At an organism or movement level we are many parts with differing roles and spiritual gifts, none more critical that the next. There are those needed to oversee administrative things, those who teach God's instructions, those who lead us in song or prayer—they are not above others, but next to all fellow servants. This is a subtle but important difference between leaders who serve with true humility and love, and hierarchical leaders who are bosses. Surely we need those who are bold to lead or to speak out, to help organize, to lead in study and encourage, but we must be careful not to worship them as we appreciate their gifts.

> *"Unless the Lord builds the house, they labor in vain who build it."* – *Psalm 127:1*

It is not our responsibility to build, maintain, or grow a successful church. Our responsibility is to be sons and daughters, to be vessels for God to flow through. It is our responsibility is to follow Christ Jesus.

FOLLOWING CHRIST

Throughout the New Testament we read Jesus saying, "follow Me," and then the disciples and multitudes of people drop what they had been occupied with to follow Him. Many are invited, but few trust and follow (see Matthew 22:14). The requirements and instructions from Christ to those who wish to follow Him are simple…do just that, follow Him. Many of us are believers, we love Jesus and the idea of following Him, but we aren't really, why?

Let's take a closer look at some of the instructions Jesus provides to ensure we know how to do so:

- He who does not take up his cross and follow after ME is not worthy of Me – Matthew 10:38.
- If anyone desires to come after Me, let him deny himself, and take up his cross daily and follow Me – Luke 9:23.
- Most assuredly, I say to you, unless one is born again, he cannot see the kingdom of God – John 3:3.

What does it mean to follow, to take up one's cross, to deny oneself or die daily, and to be born again? **Follow** (*ak-ol-oo-theh-o*), means to "be in the same way with." You must actually leave the place where you are (mentally and sometimes physically), get behind Him and walk where He walks, do what He does, think like He thinks.

In order to be able to follow, we have to take up our cross, deny ourselves, and die daily. To **die** (*ap-oth-nace-ko*) is to "die off." Our **cross** (*stow-ros*) is "self-denial," the death of our ego, and the false sense of self (self-reliance). To be **born again** (*ghen-nah-o* and *an-o-then*) means "to be regenerated from above," anew.

OUR CALL

Reviving the doctrine of Christ: What if we heard the Truth instead of old familiar lies... The ancient Church, empires and kingdoms that absorbed Christianity 300 years after Christ's ascension, strongly discouraged the use of spiritual gifts. Believers were taught that "The Church" itself was a holy, infallible entity between man and God, and that only Catholic priests could forgive, baptize, and offer salvation. Miracles were deemed acts of God's own volition and independent from man, relegating Christ followers to performing only acts of service and charity, rather than calling on God to work through them, as Jesus taught. Believers were rendered ineffective, or at least neutralized.

So, for the last fourteen hundred years the evil one has distracted believers and kept us in check. I think it is about time for this to change!

The true church, the body of believers, not Satan, holds the power over human affairs — if we exercise it. Christ delegated to us and gave us the authority needed to do what seems impossible by worldly standards. Are we failing to act upon this authority?

We are called to go out into the world and lay our hands on the sick, healing them. We are commanded to cast out demons and resurrect the dead. To preach the Gospel and baptize others in the name of the Father, the Son and the Holy Spirit. We are called to love our enemies, to selflessly love strangers and to love each other. We are called to respond to His love with our complete selves. How do we do these things? We ask, we believe, and we pray. We can do all things through Christ and nothing apart from Him. Prayer and meditation is our conscious contract with Him. It is the mechanism through which we fulfill our purpose of manifesting God, His love, light power, and grace.

I am praying for a movement across the body of believers, that all the prophets, evangelists, pastors and teachers will come together in unity of spirit, reviving the "Christianity" Jesus taught. We need to claim our true identity as His sons and daughters, learn to use the spiritual gifts He gave us, and be about equipping the saints for the work of Jesus' ministry. I hope you will join me in both prayer and action.

May we all rise up and heal the world through Christ Jesus and what He Taught. Amen

ACKNOWLEDGEMENTS

I want to thank Richie, Don and Bobby for showing me what a man who is a Christ follower does.